PRACTICAL RIBBONCRAFT

PRACTICAL RIBBONCRAFT

Christine Kingdom

PB
PARKGATE BOOKS

This edition published in 1996 by Parkgate Books Ltd

First published in Great Britain in 1994
by Anaya Publishers Ltd

1 3 5 7 9 8 6 4 2

British Library Cataloguing-in-Publication Data:
A catalogue record for this book
is available from the British Library.

ISBN 1 85585 340 X (hardback edition)
ISBN 1 85585 327 2 (paperback edition)

Editor : Julie Watkins
Designer: Patrick McLeavey, Jo Brewer
Photography: Mark Gatehouse, assisted by Sarah Rennisan
Stylist: Arabella McNee
Illustrations: Steve Dew

Colour reproduction by Typongraph s.r.l., Verona, Italy
Typeset in Great Britain by Art Photoset Ltd, Beaconsfield
Printed and bound in Hong Kong

Contents

Introduction to Ribboncraft

Where there is ribbon, there is colour and colour makes for a more interesting, more beautiful and more fulfilling environment.

Ribbons have long provided an inexpensive way of adding colour and excitement to a wardrobe or home. People have always found the luxurious appearance of ribbon very enticing; it has the almost magical ability to transform something quite ordinary into something very special. Inspiration abounds; the Victorian era, and even earlier periods in history, provide a wonderful source for today's craftsperson and you will find that many of the projects in this book have traditional roots.

Ribbons, or 'ribbands' as they were once known, have a long, long history. Since time immemorial, they have played an astonishing number of different roles, both functional and decorative; ceremonial ribbons, tokens of love and remembrance, garment fastenings and embellishment, symbols of achievement, triumph and even status. They may not be a status symbol today, but the variety of ribbons and the endless applications have never been greater.

Ribbons such as we know, did not appear until the 16th Century, and were very expensive, often interwoven with gold and silver thread. They gradually became more affordable and their popularity increased, despite the periods in history when it was illegal for anyone other than nobility to wear ribbons. Ribbons have never discriminated against age or sex; by the mid-17th century they were especially popular with men. In France and England, ribbons became the status symbol of the idle rich; how could anyone possibly work when bedecked from head to toe in such finery?

Conversely, across the Atlantic in Colonial America, very little ribbon was worn by those who held anti-English sentiments. It was not until 1815 that the first American ribbon factory came into being.

But we have entered a new age and today ribboncrafts combine rich and sumptuous texture with the modern techniques and materials available. One of my main objectives in writing this book was to highlight the wonderful range of ribbons that is now available and appropriate for so many creative crafts. Many of the ribboncraft techniques featured will be familiar to you, but perhaps when used with another medium, such as fabric, paper or embroidery silks. The techniques have been chosen to show the ribbons to their greatest effect and although they may look complex, they are deceptively simple.

The projects are designed to suit today's lifestyles; they are easy to do, satisfying to finish and stunning to look at. Nothing is difficult or complicated and no experience is necessary. You can make the projects using very different colours to those chosen and the results will be equally delightful.

There are no rules. Colours in nature often clash but still look marvellous together and this can be very exciting when interpreted through ribboncraft. Tone-on-tone colour looks very sophisticated; the careful selection of subtle colouring can give the time-worn appearance of an antique heirloom. Delicate pastels are feminine and romantic, working well in bedroom

accessories; while rich mid-tones are wonderful in living rooms as they are so restful and easy on the eye. Colour should be enjoyed. Experiment! You will find that as your design sense grows, so you will become more adventurous and develop an eye for that which works well. Look to nature, the greatest source of colour and design inspiration.

This book is all about the creation of stunning effects, using the simplest techniques and a collection of beautiful ribbons. For example, wire-edge ribbons; a joy to work with, holding the shape that the crafter dictates; sumptuous woven-edge ribbons, ideal for appliqué on garments and soft furnishings; craft ribbons for floristry and other decorative work. Satin, grosgrain, moiré, velvet, jacquard and sheer ribbon all feed the endless ideas for ribboncrafts that encompass floristry, embroidery, needlework, cake decorating and gift packaging, to name but a few.

On the following pages you will find easy to follow steps for all the most popular ribboncraft techniques and a collection of beautiful projects, many of which will become treasured heirlooms in the future. Take the ideas as you see them, or add your own creative input.

Ribbon is sold by the metre or yard and may also be purchased in pre-packed, cut lengths. If you are short on time, ready-made ribbon roses and bows are available. For projects which call for large quantities of roses or bows, they offer the added advantage of guaranteeing a uniform shape and size.

Do not be put off by the range of choice; so long as the colour, texture and style are right for your project, all you need consider is whether it must be washable, colourfast and crease resistant. You will usually find all this necessary information on the ribbon reel itself. The most important thing however, is to enjoy working with your chosen ribbon.

Roses in Ribbon

Ribbon roses can be made using a variety of techniques and the finished rose will vary accordingly. Easy to make, ribbon roses are an equally perfect trim for bridalwear or to gift wrap a present. They are all lovely; just choose the method to suit the type of ribbon used and the project that you have in mind.

Almost any ribbon can be used for making roses. Satin is sumptuous and makes up into a rich, lustrous rose that is a perfect embellishment for garments and home accessories. The sheer ribbons form beautiful, romantic cabbage roses with a soft hint of colour. By simply using two sheers together, the effect is of shot silk; the tones of colour can be as subdued or as vibrant as you wish. The vast range of colours available provides endless scope for those in search of unusual schemes.

Combine ribbon streamers, leaves or berries with roses to give added textural appeal: vary the size of the roses by simply selecting different ribbon widths; the wider the ribbon, the larger the rose. Experiment with prints and plaids, and try sheer ribbon combined with other textures, such as taffetas or satins.

The stitched rose is ideal for decorating a hat, ballgown, fashion accessory or soft furnishings, when colourfastness and washability might be necessary considerations. Providing the ribbon is washable and crease resistant, a well-made rose can be gently laundered by hand and will spring back to its former shape, as long as it was carefully and securely stitched in the first place!

A corsage, bouquet, head-dress or garland will require stemmed roses that can be wired and bound together using florist's tape. The stem should be of a heavy gauge wire that is pliable enough to make the loop and twist at the top. A finer gauge wire is used to bind the rose. Be sure to use wire cutters and craft scissors for these projects; needlework scissors would be irreparably damaged very quickly!

Use the chart below as a guide to calculate the amount of ribbon required to make roses or rosebuds, depending on the width chosen; add more ribbon for cabbage roses. Double the amount of ribbon if you work two ribbons together. The width and type of ribbon will determine the size and style of the rose, so that by mastering just one rose-making technique, you can produce a large collection of different species!

RIBBON WIDTH	STEMMED & STITCHED ROSES RIBBON LENGTH	ROSEBUDS RIBBON LENGTH
$^{3}/_{16}$in (5mm)	5in (13cm)	–
$^{1}/_{4}$in (7mm)	8in (20cm)	3in (8cm)
$^{3}/_{8}$in (9mm)	8in (20cm)	3in (8cm)
$^{5}/_{8}$in (15mm)	16in (40cm)	6in (15cm)
$^{7}/_{8}$in (23mm)	20in (50cm)	6in (15cm)
1 $^{1}/_{2}$in (39mm)	32in (80cm)	16in (40cm)
2 $^{1}/_{4}$in (56mm)	1 $^{1}/_{3}$yd (1.25m)	20in (50cm)

Stitched roses can be made in ribbon as narrow as $^{3}/_{16}$in (5mm) and $^{1}/_{4}$in (7mm), but any ribbon less than $^{5}/_{8}$in (15mm) wide is too fiddly for stemmed roses. For stemmed roses you should add approximately 4in (10cm), to allow for attaching the ribbon to the wire.

An Easy Rose in Wire-Edge Ribbon

For speed and simplicity, a wire-edge ribbon can be gathered along one side and coiled into a rose shape. These are perfect for decorating baskets and for a whole range of craft projects.

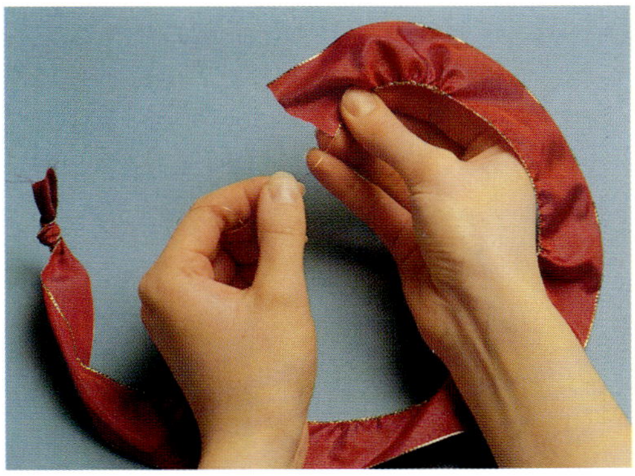

1 Take a one yard (95cm) length of wire-edge ribbon; make a knot at one end. Starting at the other end, pull up the wire from one edge only to gather gently.

2 Holding the knotted end in one hand, coil the gathered edge around the knot to form the rose.

3 Use the exposed wire to secure the raw edge at the base of the rose. A few hand stitches may help.

4 The gathered edge has formed the base; now tease the ungathered edge into the desired shape for your rose.

A Summer Hat

The hat illustrated was made using two ribbons together for each rose, but the two colours were not the same for each one. That is, a total of three tones of terracotta were used and one of chartreuse.

This summer hat was inspired by the wonderful mix of delicate hues found in frescos on the walls of beautiful summer houses in the secret gardens of stately homes; the romantic follies of days gone by. The warmth of terracotta mixed with delicate chartreuse gives depth to the soft, generous fullness of these cabbage roses.

Just one stitched rose is enough to create elegant style on a hat or ball gown, but an entire garland around the brim of a favourite straw conjures up an extravagant confection, to enjoy on special occasions or simply to bask in the summer sun.

To make each cabbage rose in two colours, you will need:
1 5/8 yd (1.50m) sheer ribbon colour 1, 2 1/4 in (56mm) wide
1 5/8 yd (1.50m) sheer ribbon colour 2, 2 1/4 in (56mm) wide
Matching thread
Needle

Stitched Rose

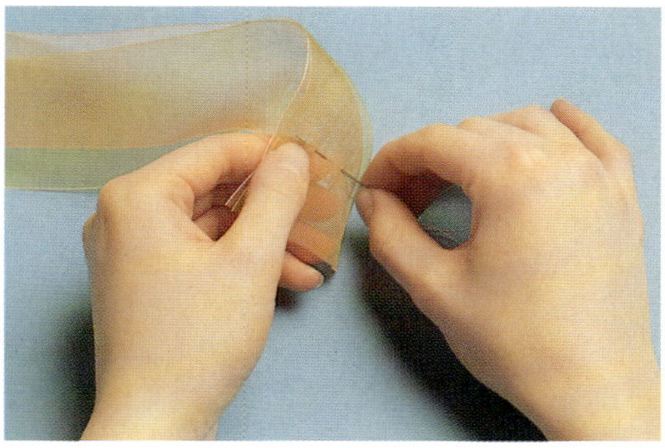

1 Holding one ribbon on top of the other, fold the ends towards you so that they lie in a vertical position and hang below the lower edge of the horizontal ribbons by about 1in (2.5cm). This will give you a handle for the ribbons as the rose is made. Make a line of stitches through all four thicknesses.

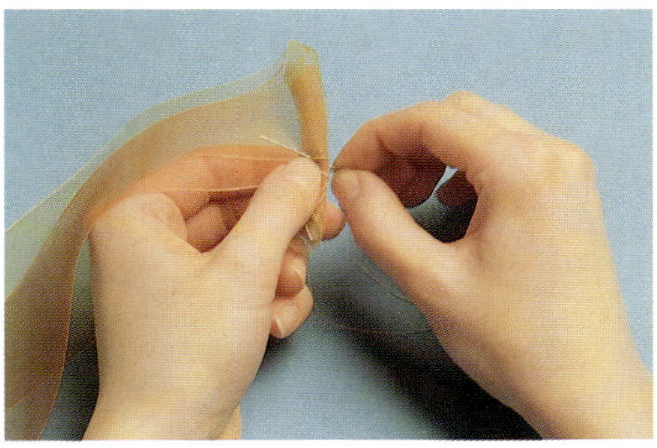

2 Working from right to left, twist the ribbon into a tube, turning about six times. Make a stitch or two at the base to secure.

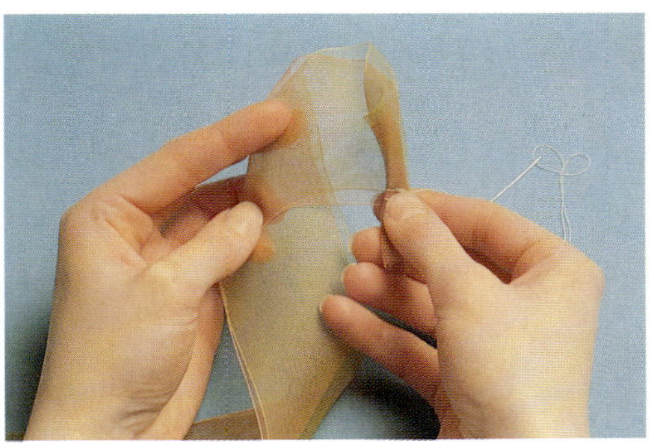

3 Leaving about $^1/_2$in (13mm) space along the top edge, fold the ribbon away from you, again forming a right angle with the ribbon ends, which are now hanging vertically. Put a pin in the bottom of the fold to hold the ribbons ready for twisting.

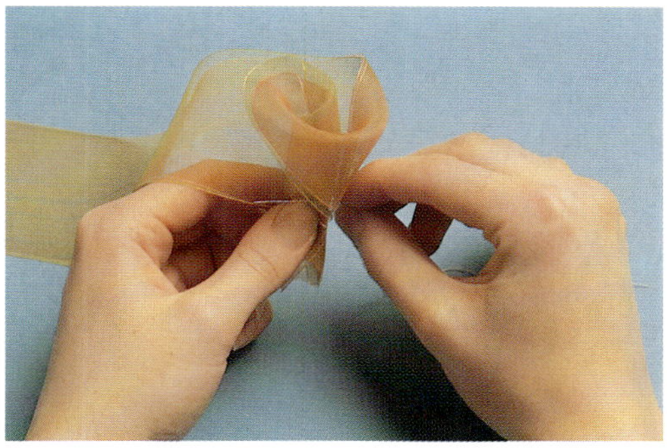

4 Twist the top edge of the bud loosely along the fold and then a little further along the top edges of the ribbon until the ribbon lengths are again running horizontally. Make a stitch to hold this section. The stitch will be higher up than the last stitch as the centre bud and twisted fold are almost level. Remove the pin.

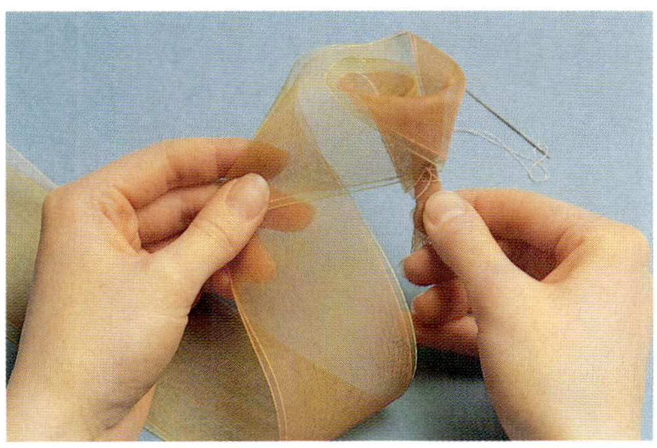

5 Leave about $^1/_2$in (13mm) along the top edge before making another fold or petal; repeat step 4. Continue in this way until you reach within 3in (7.5cm) of the ribbon ends. Fold in the usual way (step 4.) and stitch the raw edges at the base of the rose, making a small pleat or two, as necessary.

Stitch or glue the roses in place.

Cake Decorating with Stemmed Ribbon Roses

Harmonizing the cake and decorations for that special occasion could not be easier if you make roses and florist's loops in the same colour scheme that flows through the invitations, garments, table arrangements and other embellishments for the event.

The choice of cream and gold, coupled with tones of rich burgundy and pinks in a delightful mix of sheers, taffetas and gold mesh, combine beautifully together. The size of the stemmed roses and loops is determined by the scale of the project; thus narrower widths have been used to decorate the cake, while wider ones are used in the garland.

The table garland is made up of artificial ivy, which was wired together in a long length to correspond with the dimensions of the table to be adorned. Stemmed roses and ribbon loops are wired onto the ivy branches and arranged with the flowerheads facing outwards.

The cake, iced in a beautiful champagne tone, is adorned with a spray and circlet made up of stemmed roses and florist's loops. They are bound together in three stages; the top of the spray which is roughly semi-circular, the centre which is the widest part and the tail, which is tapered to a point. When each section is completed they are bound together to create one main stem, which is then placed in position on the cake and set in a holder.

Similarly, the circlet around the cake is made up in two sections; a long and a short crescent.

Remember to allow an extra 4in (10cm) of ribbon for stemmed roses.

Stemmed Roses

This technique is basically the same as that of the stitched rose, except that a wire stem is incorporated. Once you have completed a few practice roses, you will notice that each rose will be different, according to the manner in which it is wrapped. Smaller rosebuds are tightly wrapped, whereas softer, more open roses are created when you loosen the tension.

For each rose you will need:

Ribbon (refer to the chart on page 12)
Stub wire
Approximately 20in (50cm) binding wire
8in (20cm) florist's tape
Artificial rose leaves (optional)

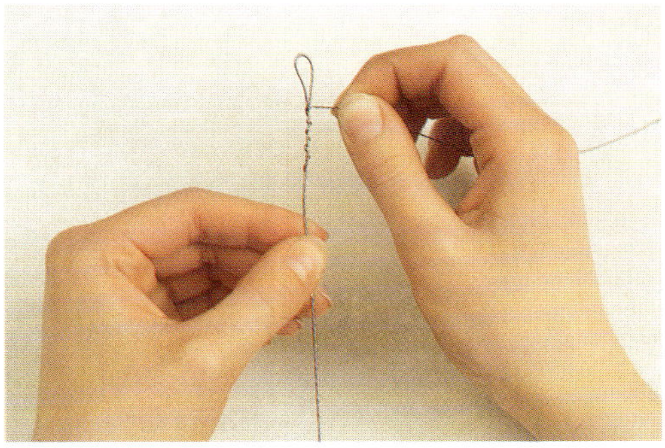

1 Make a loop in the stub wire. Thread the binding wire through the loop and twist a few times to attach securely.

2 Fold one end of the ribbon over the top of the loop and bind at the base to fix in place.

Flower Hatbox

Wire-edge ribbons can be moulded into wonderful three-dimensional shapes, as the embellishments on this purchased hat box clearly demonstrate. All it takes are a few simple stitching and folding techniques.

We chose an unusual postcard-print craft ribbon as a central band on the hat box; the colours in the design were influential in the choice of ribbons for the flowers, leaves and bows. The inclusion of iridescent taffeta ribbons in vibrant shades completes the luxurious, almost frivolous look that makes this box far too beautiful to be hidden away.

You will need:
1 $^{1}/_{3}$yd (1.25m) printed craft ribbon 5in (12.5cm) wide
2 $^{1}/_{4}$yd (2m) pink iridescent ribbon $^{7}/_{8}$in (23mm) wide
3 $^{7}/_{8}$yd (3.50m) gold iridescent ribbon $^{7}/_{8}$ in (23mm) wide
2 $^{1}/_{4}$yd (2m) turquoise iridescent ribbon $^{7}/_{8}$in (23mm) wide
1 $^{3}/_{8}$yd (1.30m) pink wire-edge iridescent ribbon 1 $^{1}/_{2}$in (39mm) wide
1 $^{3}/_{8}$yd (1.30m) gold wire-edge iridescent ribbon 1 $^{1}/_{2}$in (39mm) wide
1 $^{3}/_{8}$yd (1.30m) turquoise wire-edge iridescent ribbon 1 $^{1}/_{2}$in (39mm) wide
3 $^{1}/_{2}$yd (3.20m) willow green wire-edge taffeta ribbon 1 $^{1}/_{2}$in (39mm) wide
4yd (3.60m) green wire-edge iridescent ribbon 2 $^{1}/_{4}$in (56mm) wide

Purchased plain hat box, approximately 49in (123cm) circumference, 15 $^{3}/_{4}$in (40cm) diameter, 10 $^{1}/_{4}$in (26cm) high
1yd (95cm) plain yellow chintz fabric 54in (135cm) wide
All-purpose glue for large areas and glue gun for fixing ribbon roses
White card or felt, 15 $^{3}/_{4}$in (40cm) square
Florist's wire (optional)
Needle and thread
Pencil and ruler
Scissors
Paint

1 Paint the interior surfaces of the box with the colour of your choice.

2 Cover the hat box with the chintz. Start with the lid, using this as your template to cut the fabric. Cut a circle of chintz to cover the lid top, adding an allowance of $^{5}/_{8}$in (15mm) all the way round. Glue the chintz to the lid top. Clip into the allowance so that it will lay flat as you glue it down to the sides of the lid.

3 To trim the side of the lid; measure the depth of the lid and add 1 $^{1}/_{4}$in (30mm) for hem allowances top and bottom. Cut a piece of chintz to this depth and 49 $^{1}/_{4}$in (125cm) long. (Our fabric quantity allows for a total depth of 4 $^{1}/_{2}$in/11.5cm.) Turn under a $^{5}/_{8}$in (15mm) hem along one long edge to neaten and glue to secure. Align this edge with the upper rim of the lid. Glue the entire strip around the lid. Fold the bottom edge to the inside of the box lid and glue.

4 Cut a piece of chintz 49 $^{1}/_{4}$in x 11 $^{1}/_{2}$in (125cm x 29cm) to cover the box. Glue it in place, leaving a turning allowance of $^{5}/_{8}$in (15mm) at the top and bottom.

5 Clip into the allowance at the bottom and glue to the box base. Fold the allowance at the top over to the inside and glue. You may wish to trim this edge with craft ribbon as it will be visible.

6 Finish the box base with a circle of card or felt to conceal the raw edges. The box is now ready for decoration.

Travel in style from head to toe with this beautiful, yet functional, decorated hat box. Using simple methods and the right mix of ribbons, anyone can achieve this stunning result.

7 Lightly mark a point 1 $^{1}/_{2}$in (4cm) up from the base of the box and draw around the box at this point. This will be your guide for placing the printed craft ribbon.

8 Glue the craft ribbon in place, overlapping the ends by approximately $^{3}/_{8}$in (10mm). Try to place the join in line with the fabric join on the box.

9 Trim the side of the box lid in the same way, using the gold, $^{7}/_{8}$in (23mm) ribbon, placing the ribbon in the centre.

10 Cut twelve pieces of willow green, wire-edge ribbon; each 16cm (6 $^{3}/_{8}$in) long; and three pieces each 28cm (11in) long. Make twelve folded leaves and three stitched leaves from these lengths, following the step-by-step technique below.

11 Cut the three $^{7}/_{8}$in (23mm) ribbons into four lengths of 20in (50cm). Fold and stitch into roses, following the instructions on page 15.

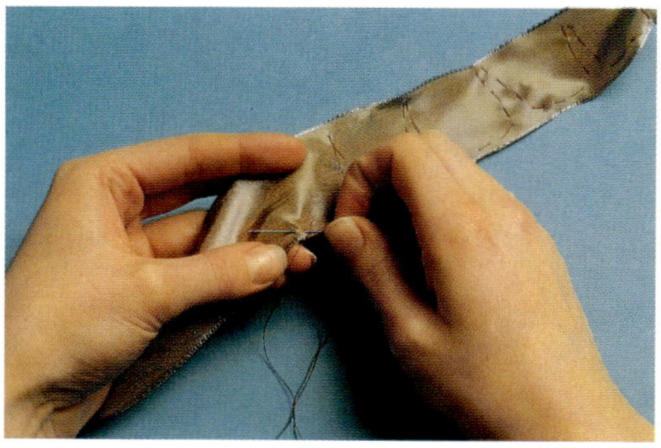

12 Take the pink, gold and turquoise wire-edge ribbons and sew a continuous series of scallop shapes, using a running stitch, along the full length of each ribbon (as illustrated).

For a realistic scallop-edged flower you should graduate the size of the petals by starting off with quite narrow scallop shapes, gradually increasing the scallop width towards the other end of the ribbon. Aim to stitch about twelve scallop shapes along the length. For an even shape, mark the ribbon into three sections and allocate a number of scallop shapes to each section, for a total of twelve.

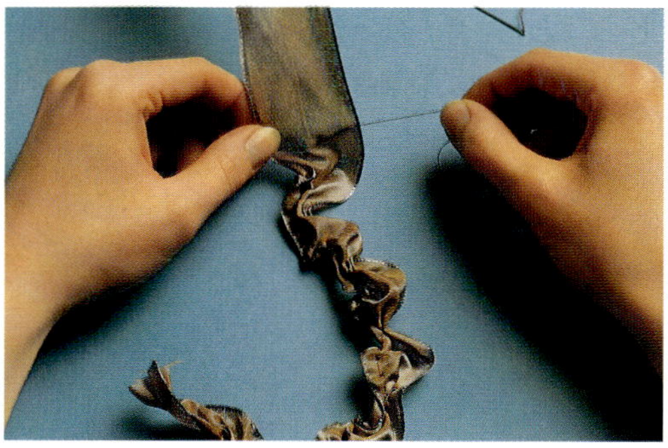

13 Gently gather both the thread and the upper wire-edge to form petals (as shown). Secure the gathering thread. Wrap the petals in a spiral, forming the flower.

The graduated scallop stitching will form quite a realistic rose, with tighter petals towards the centre, and more open petals towards the outer edges. Glue in position on the hat box.

14 To make the flower stems, twist the remaining willow wire-edge ribbon tightly and glue at each end.

15 Arrange the flowers, stems and leaves as shown, or to your own design and fix in position using the glue gun.

16 For the box top bow, cut the green wire-edge ribbon in half, giving two lengths of 2yd (1.80m) each. Fold each piece into a double bow (page 44) and wire or stitch together.

17 Wrap the centre of the bow with a 2in (5cm) scrap of ribbon and glue the join on the back. Trim each of the bow tails to a 'V'.

18 Glue the bow to the centre of the hat box lid. Arrange the bow tails and glue in place.

Folded Leaves

These can be made with most types of ribbon. Cut the ribbon to required leaf length plus allowances for neatening.

1 With the wrong side facing up, bring the ribbon ends together and fold downwards to form a centre point. Bring the outer edge of ribbon to meet the inner edge at the centre.

2 Twist along the length of the ribbon to form a stem and hand stitch to secure as shown. Wire-edge ribbon should not require stitching.

Stitched Leaves

These are more realistic when formed with wire-edge ribbons. The leaf shape can be angled, whereas other ribbons tend to give a flat or floppy appearance. Cut the ribbon to the required leaf length adding extra to neaten edges.

1 Fold the ribbon in half, wrong sides together. Make a small running stitch from one end to the other in a boat shape. The angles and depth of the boat should be adjusted according to how raised or flat you wish the leaf shape to be.

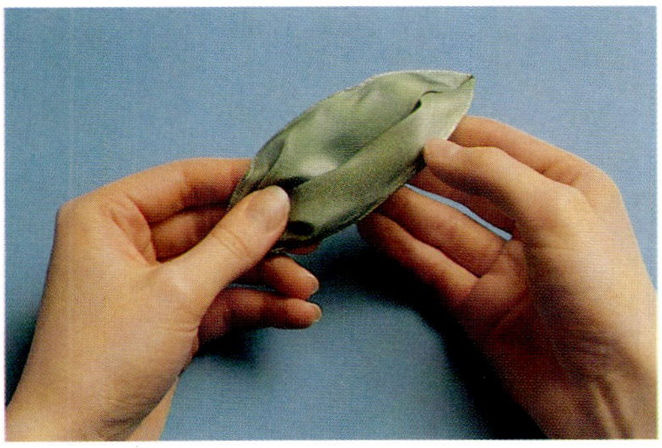

2 Turn the ribbon to the right side and mould the leaf into shape as shown. Position on the project for attachment.

Ribbons for Weaving

You can experiment with an infinite number of weaves to create interesting effects. Choose from satins, taffetas, velvets and jacquards; try incorporating lace and braids for added texture, and experiment with unusual colour combinations.

There are three basic stages in ribbon weaving; preparing the interfacing and pinning the ribbon; weaving the ribbon; bonding the ribbon to the interfacing.

The finished weave has endless applications, whatever the size. It can be made up into beautiful cushions, bedspreads and other soft furnishings, garment panels for bridalwear, christening robes, waistcoats and eveningwear. Simple shapes, such as hearts, can be woven and used as a motif for sachets and trinket boxes. Always ensure that washable woven-edge ribbons are chosen, unless you are quite confident that the finished item will never require laundering and that colour fastness is not a consideration.

The amount of ribbon required for a project will be determined by the width of the ribbon and the area to be covered. Some weaves, such as Tumbling Blocks, require more ribbon than others. However, quantities for most basic weaves are easy to calculate. Use the chart opposite to estimate ribbon quantities for your own projects, but do remember that each individual will weave to a different tension, as in knitting for example. If you weave a loose tension, you may require a little more ribbon than estimated. If working a diagonal weave, you will require more ribbon.

You will need:
Pinboard. This should be large enough to accommodate the whole piece of weaving.
Glass headed pins
Scissors
Steam iron or a dry iron used with a damp cloth
Lightweight, iron-on interfacing
Pencil/ballpoint pen
Ruler and tape measure
Ribbon

1 Prepare the interfacing for all weaving as follows:
Cut a square of interfacing to the required dimensions and add a 1in (2.5cm) allowance all the way round. Mark this seam line on the interfacing for guidance during weaving. The interfacing should always be placed on the pinboard with the adhesive side uppermost unless working with velvet (see page 34). Pin the interfacing to the pinboard, using a pin in each corner. You are now ready to start weaving.

2 Always remember the two terms used in weaving; weft refers to the horizontal ribbons, warp refers to the vertical ribbons. When pinning the warp and weft ribbons in place, always angle the pins away from the weave; it is then much easier to iron your work. You may wish to pin the bottom edge of the warp ribbons before pressing.

3 After weaving fuse or bond the ribbons to the interfacing by lightly pressing with a dry, moderate iron. Use the tip of the iron to press the ribbons at the outer edge.

4 All the pins can be removed once you are sure that the ribbons are firmly fixed in place. Turn the weaving to the wrong side and press again, this time using a moderate iron with steam or a damp cloth. Always allow the woven work to cool thoroughly before proceeding any further with your project.

RIBBON WIDTH	RIBBON REQUIRED FOR WOVEN SQUARE SIZE		
	4in (10cm)	8in (20cm)	12in (30cm)
3/16in (5mm)	6 1/2yd (6m)	22yd (20m)	45 1/2yd (42m)
1/4in (7mm)	4 1/2yd (4.20m)	15 3/4yd (14.60m)	32 3/4yd (30.20m)
3/8in (9mm)	3 1/2yd (3.40m)	12yd (11m)	25yd (23.20m)
5/8in (15mm)	2 1/4yd (2.20m)	7yd (6.60m)	15 1/4yd (14m)
7/8in (23mm)	1 1/2yd (1.40m)	5yd (4.60m)	10yd (9.20m)

The quantities given are for the entire square; if you are using more than one colour, divide the ribbon length required between the number of colours used. All quantities are given in yards and metres and include a 1in (2.5cm) seam allowance.

Weaving Techniques

Plain Weave

For a simple, 12in (30cm) square of plain weave, you will need:
5yd (4.60m) light coloured ribbon $^{7}/_{8}$in (23mm) wide
5yd (4.60m) dark ribbon $^{7}/_{8}$in (23mm) wide
14in (35cm) square of iron-on interfacing

1 Mark the seam allowance on the interfacing square, then secure to the pinboard having the adhesive side uppermost. Cut one of the ribbons into 14in (35cm) lengths. These will be the warp ribbons.

The sample weaves illustrated show techniques only; they do not relate to the ribbon lengths used for a 12in (30cm) square of weaving.

2 Pin the warp ribbons in vertical lines to the very top edge of the interfacing square. Start at the left-hand side, from the seam line. Do not overlap the ribbons but ensure they are edge-to-edge. Angle the pins away from the work to make ironing easier when you fuse the ribbons.

3 Now cut the other ribbon length into 14in (35cm) strips. These are the weft ribbons. Weave the ribbons through the warp; over the first, under the second, over the third, under the fourth and so on until you reach the other side.

4 Now push this weft ribbon up to the top seam line. Pin it at either end, well outside the seam allowance and ensuring it is taut and straight. Repeat the procedure with the next weft ribbon.

5 Continue weaving until all the weft ribbons are used. When you are quite sure that all the ribbons are correctly placed, press

and fuse the ribbons securely in place, as described in the general instructions given on page 26. You can pin the bottom edge of the warp ribbons before pressing, for greater stability.

Do not worry if you find that the last weft ribbon is lying over or beyond the bottom seam line. If, however, it is overlapping by more than $^{3}/_{8}$in (9mm), push the weft ribbons closer together or remove the last ribbon altogether.

Patchwork Weave

For a 12in (30cm) square of patchwork weave you will need:
16 $^{1}/_{4}$yd (15m) ribbon $^{1}/_{4}$in (7mm) wide colour A
7 $^{1}/_{2}$yd (7m) ribbon $^{1}/_{4}$in (7mm) wide colour B
7 $^{1}/_{2}$yd (7m) ribbon $^{1}/_{4}$in (7mm) wide colour C
14in (35cm) square of iron-on interfacing

1 Prepare the interfacing as detailed in general instructions, page 26. Cut all the ribbon into 14in (35cm) lengths.

2 Pin the warp ribbons to the top edge of the interfacing in the following colour sequence, starting from the left-hand seam line: CABA/C/ABAC.

Note: Extra sequences of CABA and ABAC can be added to either side of the central C, depending on the size of the woven piece. Adding equally to either side of C will maintain the symmetry of the weave.

3. Commencing at the top seam line on the interfacing, weave the weft ribbons in the same colour sequence as before:
Row 1 Colour C: Over 2, under 1, over 3, under 1; repeating to the end.
Row 2 Colour A: Under 2, over 2, under 2, over 2; repeating to the end.
Row 3 Colour B: Over 1, under 1, over 1, under 1, over 1; repeating to the end.
Row 4 Colour A: Under 1, over 2, under 2, over 2, under 2; repeating to the end.
Repeat the entire sequence until you reach the bottom seam line. You may have some ribbon lengths left over at the end.

4. Bond the ribbons to the interfacing, following the general instructions, detailed on page 26.

Zigzag Weave

The best effect in this weave is achieved by using just two different colours. Vary this effect with different ribbon widths.

To weave a 12in (30cm) zigzag square you will need:
16 $^{3}/_{4}$yd (15.40m) ribbon $^{1}/_{4}$in (7mm) wide colour A (light blue)
16yd (14.70m) ribbon $^{1}/_{4}$in (7mm) wide colour B (navy)
14in (35cm) square of iron-on interfacing

1 Prepare the interfacing as detailed on page 26 and cut all the ribbons into lengths of 14in (35cm). As usual, starting at the left-hand seam line, pin the warp ribbons, in alternating colours, to the very top edge of the interfacing.

2 Weave the weft ribbon in the following sequence, starting at the top seam line on the left-hand side of the interfacing square:
Row 1 Colour A: Under 2, over 2 - repeat to the end.
Row 2 Colour B: Under 1, over 2, under 2, over 2 - repeat, in two's, to the end.
Row 3 Colour A: Over 2, under 2, over 2 - repeating to the end, in two's.
Row 4 Colour B: Over 1, under 2, over 2, under 2 - repeating in two's, to the end.
Repeat the sequence until the square is completed.

3 Bond or fuse the ribbon weaving to the interfacing, following the general instructions on page 26.

Tumbling Blocks Weave

This design, also known as Baby Blocks or the Box Pattern, was a favourite patchwork and quilting pattern throughout the 19th Century and was made up into a variety of domestic furnishings, including cushions, chair seats and foot stools.

Weaving three different colours, often a dark, medium and light tone, the optical illusion of a three-dimensional box created by this technique can be used to full effect; subtle or high impact. When repeated over an area, the appearance is of a whole stack of blocks rather like a child's building bricks.

The design has been cleverly woven in ribbon in the two stages shown. The first stage is a conventional warp and weft format. In the second stage a slightly narrower ribbon is woven diagonally through the warp and weft. Tumbling Blocks lends itself to an eclectic mix of satins, grosgrains and jacquards in brilliant colours.

For a 30cm (12in) square you will need:
5 $^{1}/_{8}$yd (4.60m) ribbon $^{7}/_{8}$in (23mm) wide in a light colour for the warp
5 $^{1}/_{8}$yd (4.60m) ribbon $^{7}/_{8}$in (23mm) wide in a dark shade for the weft
8 $^{1}/_{4}$yd (7.60m) ribbon $^{5}/_{8}$in (15mm) wide in toning shades for the diagonal weave
14in (35cm) square iron-on interfacing

1 Prepare the interfacing as you would for all weaving. Cut the warp and weft ribbons into 14in (35cm) lengths; you should have thirteen in each colour.

2 Pin the warp ribbons to the top edge of the interfacing. Make sure they are all edge-to-edge, but not overlapping at all. Work from the left-hand side seam line which should be marked on the interfacing.

3 Commencing at the top seam line, weave the weft ribbons in the following pattern:
Row 1: Over 1, under 1, over 2, under 1 and repeat to the end.
Row 2: Under 1, over 2, under 1, over 2 and repeat to the end.
Row 3: Over 2, under 1, over 2, under 1 and repeat to the end.

Repeat the entire sequence for all warp and weft ribbons, placing them as close together as possible.

4 Now take the diagonal weave ribbon in one complete length. You may find it easier to weave if you attach a safety pin to the lead end of the ribbon.

Start the diagonal weave from the bottom right-hand edge, feeding the ribbon over the first two weft (navy) ribbons, then under the next two warp (light blue) ribbons; over the next two weft (navy) ribbons, continuing the sequence up to the top left-hand corner.

Note: You may find it necessary to remove temporarily a pin from the edge as you weave; do not forget to replace it before going on to the next diagonal.

5 Pull the ribbon over the last warp and lay it on the interfacing. Pin it in place. Once you have checked that the diagonal is taut and straight, you can pin down the other end and then cut the ribbon.

6 Continue the diagonal weaving, working above the line you have just completed. Finally, weave the diagonals below your starting point in the same way. You may wish to use a second colour for the diagonal weave (as we have here) for added dimension.

Note: If you work Tumbling Blocks in a rectangle, you will find that the diagonals will finish slightly off-set in the opposite corner to where you started; they cannot follow the true diagonals of a rectangle.

7 Fuse the ribbons to the interfacing, ensuring first that the weave is completely smooth and taut. Follow the pressing instructions on page 26.

Patchwork Cushion

The combination of plain and printed satins in different widths forms a patchwork effect on this decorative cushion. Colours can be selected to co-ordinate with other soft furnishings in your favourite room. Back the cushion with toning fabric.

Use your ribbon weaving skills to enhance many aspects of the home.

You will need:
3 $^{1}/_{2}$yd (3.2m) patterned ribbon (No 1) $^{7}/_{8}$in (23mm) wide
2 $^{5}/_{8}$yd (2.4m) patterned ribbon (No 2) $^{7}/_{8}$in (23mm) wide
16yd (14.4m) plain ribbon (No 3) $^{3}/_{8}$in (9mm) wide
One 16 $^{1}/_{4}$in (41cm) square of iron-on interfacing
One 16 $^{1}/_{4}$in (41cm) square of silk to back the cushion
20in (50cm) contrasting silk fabric 45in (115cm) wide
1 $^{3}/_{4}$yd (1.60m) piping cord
10in (25cm) zip
One cushion pad 15in (38cm) square

Note: A $^{5}/_{8}$in (15mm) seam allowance has been included on all fabric requirements.

1 Place the interfacing on a board with the adhesive side uppermost. Mark out a square on the interfacing, leaving a $^{5}/_{8}$in (15mm) seam allowance around the outer edge. Cut the three ribbons into 16in (40cm) lengths.

2 Starting at the left side of the board, pin the warp ribbons onto the interfacing in the following order: 1 x No 1, 3 x No 3, 1 x No 2, 3 x No 3, 1 x No 1, 3 x No 3, 1 x No 2, 3 x No 3, 1 x No 1, 3 x No 3, 1 x No 2, 3 x No 3, 1 x No 1.

3 Weave the weft ribbons in the same order as the warp ribbons, starting at the top of the board. Pin them in place at each end, inserting the pins at an angle, away from the weave. When the square is complete, check that the ribbons are smooth and straight. Re-arrange them if necessary.

4 Using a moderate, dry iron, press the weave lightly whilst it is still attached to the board. This will bond the ribbons to the interfacing. Carefully remove the weave from the board and steam press on the wrong side, that is, on the interfacing side, to secure firmly the ribbons to the interfacing.

5 Cut a 1 $^{1}/_{4}$in (3cm) strip of contrasting silk fabric on the bias to edge the entire cushion, joining the strips where necessary. Press the seams flat. Enclose the piping cord in the silk bias and tack the raw edges together. Place the raw edges of the piping to the raw edges of the cushion front, woven side uppermost, and tack in place.

6 With right sides together, sew the cushion front and back together around all edges, leaving a 10in (25cm) gap along one edge for the zip. Turn to the right side and press lightly. Hand stitch the zip in place.

Victorian Purse

Velvet gives a wonderfully rich effect when used in combination with taffetas and other textures. Very delicate ribbons or those which have a pile, such as velvet, can be woven from the wrong side to avoid any damage to the ribbon texture. This zigzag weave was worked on the reverse face and without the use of interfacing during the weaving process.

The colours chosen for this project are the dark, natural colours associated with Victoriana. The finished length of the purse is 8in (20cm). All ribbons used are $^1/_4$in (7mm) wide.

You will need:
3 $^1/_4$yd (3m) moss green velvet ribbon
3 $^1/_4$yd (3m) purple velvet ribbon
3 $^1/_4$yd (3m) wine red velvet ribbon
3 $^1/_4$yd (3m) black velvet ribbon
12 $^3/_4$yd (11.70m) black taffeta ribbon
Antique gold silk lining fabric 9x22in (23x56cm)
Iron-on interfacing 9x17in (23x43cm) (Grey interfacing will not show through the fabric)
5in (13cm) square of black velvet fabric

For the purse tie: 2yd (1.80m) of $^1/_8$in (3mm) doubleface satin ribbon in the following colours; purple, wine red and black.

1 Cut all four velvet ribbons into thirteen equal lengths, each approximately 9in (23cm) long. Cut the taffeta ribbon into 27 lengths, each approximately 17in (43cm) long.

2 Pin the velvet ribbons in vertical lines to the pinboard. Ensure the velvet pile is facing the pinboard and leave a small gap of approximately $^{1}/_{16}$in (1mm) between each. Use the following colour sequence, repeating until all ribbons are laid down: black, red, purple and green.

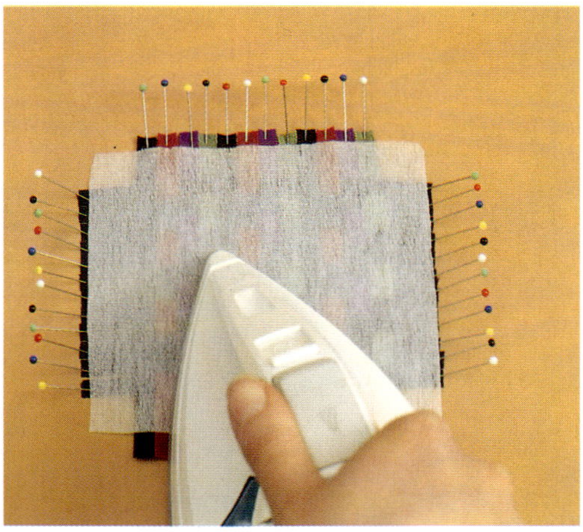

3 Leaving a $^{5}/_{8}$in (15mm) seam allowance at the top, weave the taffeta ribbon across the velvets using a diagonal weave. When weaving is complete, take the interfacing and place the adhesive down to the wrong side of the ribbons. Press with a moderate, dry iron to secure the ribbons to the interfacing. Remove the pins and press again on the wrong side only. You should only press on the right side if you feel it is possible to do so without damaging the ribbons.

4 With right sides facing, bring the two short edges together and stitch, taking a $^{5}/_{8}$in (15mm) seam allowance.

5 Cut a circle 5in (13cm) in diameter from the velvet fabric and stitch this to one end of the tube, to form the base. Stitch with right sides together, taking a $^{5}/_{8}$in (15mm) seam allowance.

6 Cut a circle as above and a rectangle (9x17in/23x43cm) from the lining material and make up as detailed in Step 5.

7 With right sides together, place the velvet purse inside the lining purse. Machine stitch the two together around the upper edge, leaving an opening of 2in (5cm). Turn through to the right side and close the opening with small, invisible stitches.

8 Make a channel for the tie at the top of the purse by stitching two lines, through all layers, either side of the seventh and eighth ribbon.

9 Cut each of the $^{1}/_{8}$in (3mm) ribbons into three equal lengths. Taking each colour individually, twist the ribbons in a clockwise direction along their entire length. Then twist all three cords together in an anti-clockwise direction. Bind the tie with black sewing thread, approximately 1 $^{1}/_{2}$in (4cm) from each end. Thread the tie through the channel, starting and finishing opposite the side seam.

Ribbons and Bows

To tie ribbon in a decorative fashion opens up a great many possibilities for the inventive. Ribbon is one of the most widely used materials for embellishment of clothing, soft furnishings, gifts, floristry and handicrafts and, more often than not, that ribbon is fashioned in a bow.

Whatever your taste and style; be it romantic and ethereal as the sheers in delicate pastels, the drama of bold, strong colours and prints, or the country-fresh look of mid-tonal floral prints, checks and stripes, you can create bows that blend perfectly into your design scheme. A bow adds dimension, showing off the lustrous texture and beauty of the ribbon. Let your imagination be your guide, the style you choose reflecting your personal taste.

Opportunities and occasions for making bows occur constantly. Christmas; a time when the bow comes into its own, making a stunning decoration for wreaths, table arrangements, the tree and gifts. Whether you choose a traditional theme in plaids and old gold, or the opulence of rich jewel colours with lots of glitz, both look brilliant in the right setting. For weddings the delicious colours in satins and sheers make glorious bows with long, floaty tails for bridal gowns and bridesmaids circlets. Smaller, less flamboyant versions make dainty decorations for the invitations and even the cake. For a young, contemporary style, try a brightly coloured wire-edge taffeta or a gingham check.

From the narrowest $^1/_{16}$in (1.5mm) ribbon to the widest 3 $^1/_4$in (80mm) ribbon, bows add a finishing touch in a multitude of sizes and styles. A pale pink or blue mini bow is a pretty trim on a baby's layette, while a large, overstated multi-loop bow in a strong colour adds a festive finish to a gift hamper full of tasty goodies.

Satin ribbon often comes to mind as a first choice for bows, but do not overlook sheers, wire-edge taffetas, prints, lurex and other novelty ribbons. You can have lots of fun putting together different colours and widths, either working them in layers or making separate bows and then layering them for a tiered effect. As a general rule, if the ribbon will make a tight knot in the centre when you tie it, then it is suitable for use in a bowmaker or for hand-tying. If it is too stiff, then you will need to use either a binding wire, or pleat and stitch the centre to achieve a good shape.

The tails are as important to a bow's appearance as the loops. If you are unsure about the tail length, plan them longer; you can always cut them shorter if necessary. Finish the ends diagonally or in an inverted 'V'. This not only looks attractive but also prevents a woven ribbon from fraying.

Bows can be deceptive; they usually take more ribbon than expected as you need to allow ease in the loop construction. Generally, bows made on a bowmaker are easier to manipulate, leaving your hands free to fashion the tails, keeping the right side facing out. You have less control with a hand-tied bow but you can always put a few stitches at the back of the bow once tying is completed. This will help to stabilize the centre and maintain the loop and tail positions.

It seems then, that there is always a reason to tie a bow. The following chapter will teach you how to make simple bows in such a way that they look both spectacular and unique.

Bow Techniques

When you first venture into the art of bowmaking, the number of style variations can be a little daunting. Here is a quick summary of the different types, but first let us identify the basic components of a bow.

The Hand-Tied Single Loop Bow

The entire bow, including the centre knot, is tied from just one continuous piece of ribbon. There are no wires or separate strips of ribbon required. Likewise, no stitching or gluing is involved. This is a classic bow which can be used for gift wrapping, garment trimming and decorating craft projects.

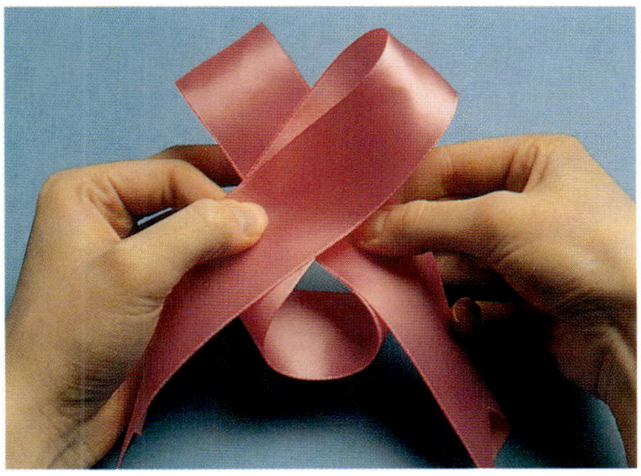

1 Take a length of ribbon. Fold it in half. Divide each half again to give you a loop and tail in each hand. You should adjust the ribbon now for longer/shorter tails or bigger/smaller loops. Fold the left loop over the right.

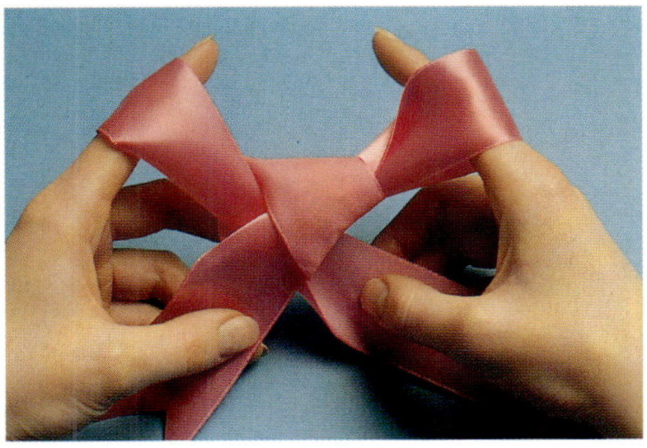

2 Take the left loop round to the back and through the centre hole. Pull the centre tight, adjusting as necessary to make loops and tails equal in size.

Bowmaker Bows

If you find hand-tied bows quite difficult and even exasperating to make, then you will almost certainly take great delight in owning a bowmaker. A simple, but highly effective tool, the bowmaker allows you to make perfect bows every time, whatever the width of ribbon, number of loops, or quantity required. It is particularly helpful for the tiny bows used for cake and stationery decorating, which are usually so fiddly to make by hand. Full instructions for a variety of bows are included with the tool. See Stockists and Suppliers, page 124, for details of where to purchase your bowmaker.

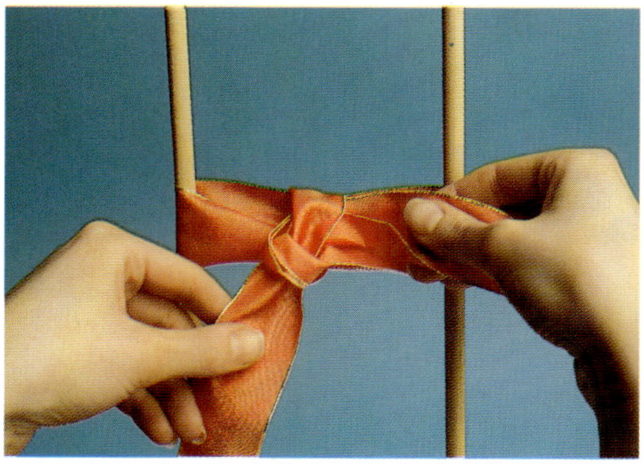

In the second category of bows, the ribbon is folded to a certain format and then bound in the centre with a wire, or stitched. For example, the Double Loop Bow, the Pompom and Florist's Loops.

Generally, if the wire or stitching is visible when the bow has been completed, a separate short strip of ribbon is used to cover the centre and then glued or stitched at the centre back.

Double and Multi-Loop Bows

These are made from a continuous single length of ribbon which is folded into the desired number of loops. It is then either stitched or wired through the centre.

Pompoms

Create an extravagant, frothy bow with a series of loops secured with wire. Like the Double Bow, the Pompom is made from a single length of ribbon. Allow about 2 $^{1}/_{4}$yd (2m) of ribbon for an average bow; you will need less for small pompoms, and more for large. This bow is best suited to craft (cut-edge) ribbon and the narrower sheers; woven-edge ribbons such as satins, are not suitable.

1 Start with a loop of ribbon equal to the diameter of the finished bow, in this case, about 6in (15cm) across.

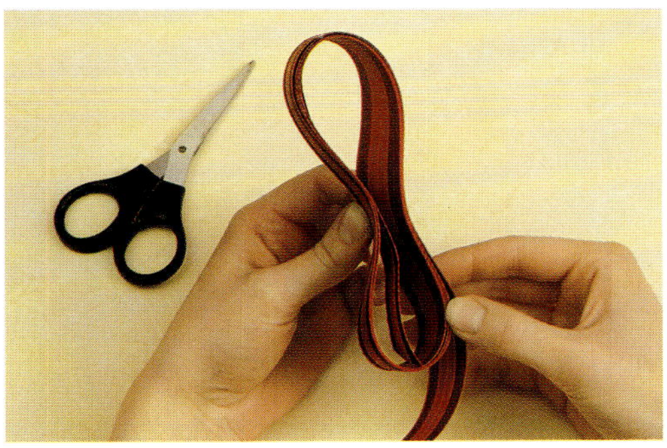

2 Wrap the ribbon around this first loop about ten times, or until all the ribbon is used.

3 Flatten the loops so that you have a rectangle. Cut the corners diagonally, taking care not to cut too close to the centre.

4 Carefully bring the cut corners together to meet at the middle; the middle of the ribbon now forms the 'neck' of the bow.

5 Wrap the wire around the middle and pull out the loops, twisting them in different directions as you pull them out. Trim the ribbon ends.

Use this bow to embellish that wonderful gift that is too big to wrap!

Florist's Loops

These can be any length or width, to suit the project, such as the cake on page 18. To make a florist's loop, simply divide the ribbon into the required number of loops and tails.

1 For a double loop and tails, as pictured here, divide the ribbon into six equal sections along the length. Fold the ribbon concertina-style, pinching the folds together at the base between thumb and forefinger.

2 Bind the base of the ribbon securely with wire. Fold the two ends of wire down to an equal length, thereby forming a stem for the loop. Twist the wire ends together and bind with florist's tape for a neat finish.

In the third group, the bow is made up in sections; the loops, the tails and the centre. For example, tiered or layered bows are made in this way.

Tiered Bows

The tiered and layered bows are formed by simply laying several single loops on top of one another, grading the loop size. You will need a short piece of ribbon to go around the centre and a length for the ribbon tails. For the basic single loop follow steps 1 and 2 below.

1 Cut a piece of ribbon to twice the required finished width of the bow. Add 2in (5cm) for a seam allowance and ease. Overlap and stitch the raw ends to form a loop.

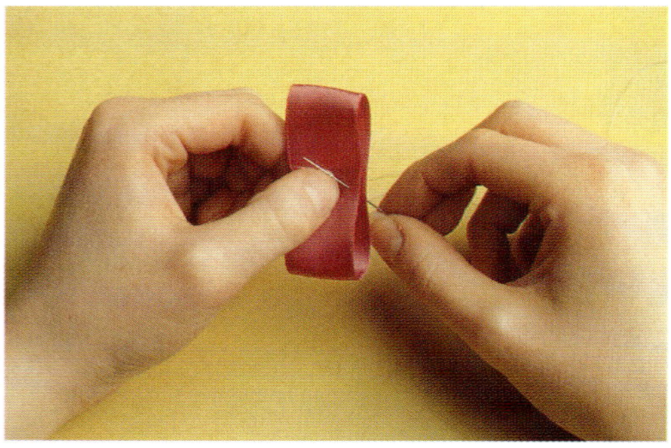

2 Place the join at the centre back and flatten the loop slightly. Pinch the edges together at the centre and either stitch or secure with glue.

3 Cut the next length of ribbon slightly shorter. The exact measurement will depend on the effect you require. Make the loop in the same way and place it on top of the first.

4 Continue with more loops, grading each loop in size if you wish. To save time, stitch the layered bow through the centre when all the layers are in place. Finish the layered bow by concealing the stitching or glue with a short piece of ribbon. Wrap this around the centre, ensuring raw edges are turned in, and secure it at the back.

Tails can be added to the back of a tiered bow; simply glue or sew two lengths of ribbon in place, positioning them at an angle to achieve the right effect.

In the fourth category of bows we have folded ribbon to give attractive shapes, for example, the Figure-of-Eight bow, finished by gluing or stitching.

Figure-of-Eight Bow

1 Find the centre in a length of ribbon. Hold this spot under your thumb. Twist the ribbon in a figure-of-eight, creating equal-sized pointed loops. Tuck the ribbon under your thumb each time it crosses the centre.

2 Continue until you have four completed loops.

3 Adjust the position of the loops if necessary. Stitch in place at the centre point.

4 A four-pointed Figure-of-Eight can be applied to another, thus giving an eight-pointed rosette effect.

Gift Packaging

The desire to transform ordinary things into magical gifts gives pleasure to all. For those who enjoy wrapping parcels, the potential for ribbon embellishment is tremendous. It adds an air of mystery to the gift; the giver knows what is inside the parcel, the recipient does not. The point of the exercise is to provide a frisson of excitement for both parties involved, making something special out of what might otherwise be mundane. The richness of the wrappings, ribbon flounces and furbelows are a delight to the eye and lift the spirit.

The following projects can look quite different worked in alternative colour schemes. Choose jewel colours for a festive trim and neutral tones for a sophisticated, natural style.

Attach the base of the bow to a small square of card for easy application to parcels and decorated projects.

Shaded Roses

You will need:
1 $^{1}/_{8}$yd (1m) cream polyester twill ribbon 1 $^{1}/_{2}$in (39mm) wide
1 $^{1}/_{8}$yd (1m) cream sheer ribbon with satin stripe 1 $^{1}/_{2}$in (39mm) wide
1 $^{1}/_{8}$yd (1m) soft green polyester twill ribbon $^{1}/_{2}$in (12mm) wide
18in (46cm) tan polyester twill ribbon $^{7}/_{8}$in (23mm) wide
18in (46cm) cream polyester twill ribbon $^{7}/_{8}$in (23mm) wide
Beige card 1in x 2in (2.5cm x 5cm) (optional)
Needle and matching thread
Fine florist's wire
All-purpose glue

1 With the sheer ribbon overlaying the 1 $^{1}/_{2}$in (39mm) cream twill ribbon, fold the two into a double bow and stick onto the card. Trim the four ribbon ends.

2 Make two ribbon roses from each of the $^{7}/_{8}$in (23mm) twill ribbons and glue them to the middle of the large bow.

3 Cut the $^{1}/_{2}$in (12mm) green ribbon into four equal lengths. Make four florist's loops, each having two loops and two tails. Bind the base with thread, not wire.

4 Glue two either side of the roses so that the tails and loops cascade outwards.

Eight-Petal Puff Ball

You will need:
1 $^{3}/_{8}$yd (1.25m) tan polyester twill ribbon 1 $^{1}/_{2}$in (39mm) wide
24in (60cm) cream sheer ribbon with satin stripe 1 $^{1}/_{2}$in (39mm) wide
Beige card 1in x 2in (2.5cm x 5cm)
Needle and matching thread
Fine florist's wire
All-purpose glue

1 Cut the tan ribbon into two lengths measuring 27in (68cm) and 22 $^{1}/_{2}$in (57cm). Fold the longer length into a figure-of-eight bow. Holding the centre firmly in the fingers, fold a second figure-of-eight alongside.

2 Ensure the four loops or petals are even in size before stitching them through the centre and gluing to the card.

3 Make four similar, but smaller, figure-of-eight loops with the second length of tan ribbon. Secure with a few stitches through the middle then position in the middle of the larger petals. Glue in place.

4 Cut the sheer ribbon into five equal lengths. Fold each into a loop. Stitch or wire the ends together. Glue one loop in each of the four outer petals, placing the fifth loop in the centre of the bow to complete.

Golden Beechnuts

You will need:
1 $^{3}/_{8}$yd (1.25m) gold sheer metallic chevron ribbon $^{5}/_{8}$in (15mm) wide
32in (80cm) gold-edged, cream taffeta ribbon $^{5}/_{8}$in (15mm) wide
10 $^{1}/_{4}$in (26cm) chocolate brown doubleface satin ribbon $^{1}/_{8}$in (3mm) wide
Beige card 1in x 2in (2.5cm x 5cm)
Four beechnuts
Four allspice (dried pimento) sprayed gold
Short cinnamon sticks
Fine florist's wire
All-purpose glue

1 Cut a 32in (80cm) length of the metallic ribbon, overlay it on the cream taffeta and fold a double bow. Wire the centre. Cut the ends at a slant and glue to the card.

2 Glue the beechnuts centrally, adding an allspice to the middle of each. Fold the brown ribbon into a double bow; position and glue amongst the beechnuts.

3 Cut the remaining metallic ribbon into two equal lengths and make two florist's loops, each having two loops and two tails. Bind each base with thread and insert at the base of the beechnuts. Glue in place.

4 Arrange short lengths of cinnamon sticks in and around the beechnuts. Glue to secure.

Shades of Bronze

You will need:
33in (83cm) copper metallic ribbon 2 $^{3}/_{4}$in (70mm) wide
4 $^{3}/_{4}$in (12cm) copper grosgrain metallic ribbon 1 $^{1}/_{2}$in (39mm) wide
Three small sprigs of glycerined ruscus leaves or small, dried leaves of your choice
Beige card 1in x 2in (2.5cm x 5cm)
Needle and matching thread
Fine florist's wire
All-purpose glue

1 Fold the wider metallic ribbon into a double bow, securing it with wire in the middle. Cut the ends at a slant, then glue to the card.

2 Divide the grosgrain ribbon into two equal lengths. Fold the upper corners of each to the centre to form a pointed petal and stitch to hold in place.

3 Glue the two grosgrain petals, base towards base, to the centre of the metallic bow.

4 Glue a ruscus sprig to either side of the grosgrain petals, and place the remaining sprig in the middle to conceal the join.

Pleated Folds

You will need:
12 $^{3}/_{4}$in (32cm) tan polyester twill ribbon 1 $^{1}/_{2}$in (39mm) wide
8 $^{1}/_{2}$in (22cm) cream polyester twill ribbon 1 $^{1}/_{2}$in (39mm) wide
15in (38cm) tan polyester twill ribbon $^{7}/_{8}$in (23mm) wide
7in (18cm) cream polyester twill ribbon $^{7}/_{8}$in (23mm) wide
Beige card 1in x 2in (2.5cm x 5cm)
Needle and matching thread
All-purpose glue

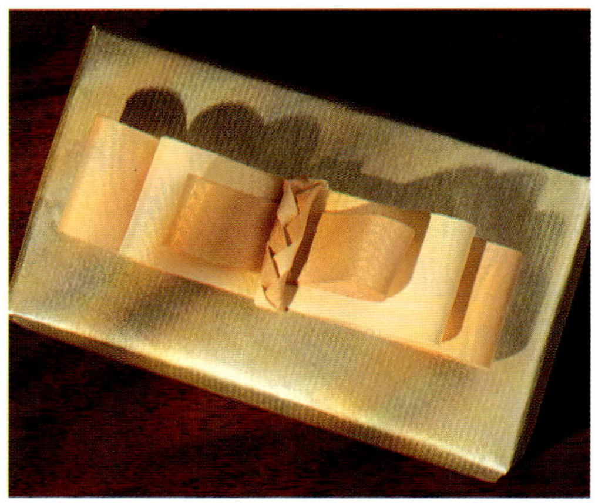

1 Using the tiered bow method, make two loops using the wider width tan and cream ribbons. Glue the cream loop on top of the tan loop.

2 Cut a 8in (20cm) length of $^{7}/_{8}$in (23mm) tan ribbon. Make a loop and glue as before. Stick this on top of the other two loops.

3 Now cut the remaining $^{7}/_{8}$in (23mm) tan ribbon in half lengthways. Fold each strip in half again and press using a warm iron and damp cloth. You should now have two folded strips approximately $^{3}/_{16}$in (5mm) wide.

4 Repeat this step with the $^{7}/_{8}$in (23mm) cream ribbon.

5 Discard one cream folded strip and plait the remaining cream strip with the two tan strips. Place the finished plait over the middle of the prepared bow and stitch it neatly at the back to secure. Glue the completed bow to the card.

Golden Star

You will need:
26in (66cm) sandstone doubleface satin ribbon $^{7}/_{8}$in (23mm) wide
26in (66cm) sheer, gold metallic chevron-striped ribbon $^{5}/_{8}$in (15mm) wide
27 $^{1}/_{2}$in (70cm) sheer, gold metallic-striped ribbon $^{3}/_{16}$in (5mm) wide
5 $^{1}/_{2}$in (14cm) sheer, gold metallic chevron-striped ribbon 1 $^{1}/_{2}$in (39mm) wide
5 $^{1}/_{2}$in (14cm) plain gold metallic ribbon 2 $^{3}/_{4}$in (70mm) wide
Beige card 1in x 2in (2.5cm x 5cm)
Needle and matching thread
All-purpose glue

1 Lay the $^{5}/_{8}$in (15mm) metallic chevron ribbon on top of the $^{7}/_{8}$in (23mm) satin. Fold and stitch a double bow, cutting the four ribbon ends at a slant. Glue this bow to the beige card.

2 Cut the $^{3}/_{16}$in (5mm) ribbon into two equal lengths; fold each into a florist's loop having four loops and four tails. Bind each base with thread and glue them to the card, on either side of the large bow.

3 Cut the 1 $^{1}/_{2}$in (39mm) ribbon into two equal lengths. Cut one end of each piece at a slant. Insert the square ends diagonally beneath the main bow and glue in place.

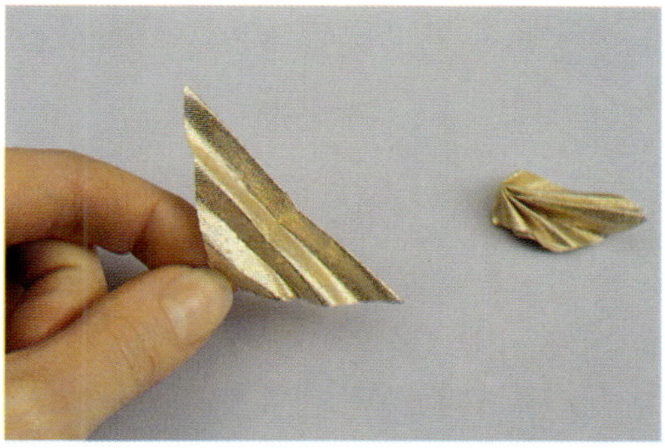

4 Cut the 2 $^{3}/_{4}$in (70mm) gold ribbon into two equal lengths, thus forming two small squares. Fold each square into a triangle. Starting at the apex, make concertina pleats in the ribbon. Finger press firmly.

5 Fold the two base ends together to form a pair of pleated wings; catchstitch neatly to hold the shape. Glue the wings to the middle of the bow.

A word of caution; when selecting your ribbon, keep your project in mind; will the ribbon pleat, will it fray if cut?

Table Centrepiece

Entertaining at home can be fun, rewarding and, with a little extra care, a feast for the eye as well as the palate! Simple details such as a decorative centrepiece or place setting can add to the sense of occasion.

Entwine stemmed ribbon roses around crisp white napkins or tie miniature bows around individually-wrapped gifts for special guests and occasions.

Colour co-ordinate a decorative centrepiece with your dinner service and linen. The style of the centrepiece will largely depend on the mood you are trying to create. For very casual events the look will be as natural as possible, while more formal occasions deserve a more elaborate decoration in which ribbons abound. Do not be tempted to create a centrepiece which is too tall or angular and therefore a barrier to conversation.

This arrangement is very easy to make and, by varying the fruits, berries, flowers and foliage, it can be adapted for every season and occasion.

You will need:
Approximately 4 $^3/_8$yd (4m) ribbon $^7/_8$in or 1 $^1/_2$in (23mm or 39mm) wide, type and colour to suit the occasion
One 8 or 10in (20 or 25cm) diameter basket, terracotta pot, or any other suitable container
Dry oasis to fill the container
Pebbles to weight the container
Moss or lichen to cover the oasis
12in (30cm) medium gauge florist's wire stems
A selection of artificial berries, pine cones, pine twigs, foliage and/or dried flowers to suit the design scheme
One large candle, approximately 10in high × 1 $^1/_2$in in diameter (25 × 3.9cm)

1 Place the pebbles in the pot. Fill the pot with oasis and cover with moss. Fold four or five wire stems in half to form long pins. Use these to secure the moss on top of the oasis. Bind wires around the cones, twigs and berries to create stems. Make the ribbon up into large florist's loops adding a wire stem (see page 46 for the technique). You are now ready to make the arrangement.

2 Place the berries, flower heads and cones evenly around the pot so that there is colour and interest from every angle. Fill in the spaces with pine twigs and/or foliage of your choice. Position the candle securely in the centre and finish with the placement of the florist's loops.

A centrepiece using fresh flowers and foliage can be created in a similar manner. Substitute pre-soaked oasis which can be concealed with a variety of greenery, instead of moss, when the arrangement is firmly in place.

Christmas Wreath

It is always a very special moment when the time comes to bring out the Christmas decorations. How much more special it is when they are imaginative decorations which you have crafted yourself! Much of the pleasure comes from rediscovering the decorations which were packed away the previous year, or creating special new decorations to add to the family collection.

All areas of the home can be festooned with ribbon; from the front door wreath which first welcomes visitors, to the beautifully adorned tree and attractive candle arrangements.

It is interesting to note the significance of the evergreen wreath and candlelight; they have a deeper history than you might imagine. Decorating the house with such items at the end of each year was traditional long before Christianity began. For many pagan peoples the Winter Solstice marked the turn of the year, reminding them that Spring would soon be on the way. Evergreens were used for decoration, symbolizing fertility as the days lengthened and the sun grew stronger; bringing a renewal of life and growth, the promise of fresh crops. The Romans used wreaths and garlands to decorate their homes in December. A three-day festival was presided over by Streniz, the goddess of Health. Gifts of greenery, wound into wreaths, were exchanged and fixed to the household door, ensuring health for the coming year.

You can use fresh or dried material to make festive wreaths. Select the entwining ribbon to echo the theme of your Christmas tree or other festive decorations around the home. The traditional colours of tartan always look good and complement berries, greenery and fir cones. A bow gives the finishing touch and can be an elaborate multi-loop or a more simple design, using a hand-tied or wired bow. All these techniques are covered on pages 43–47. The amount of ribbon that you need will depend upon the size of the wreath and how dominant you wish the ribbon decoration to be.

Cinnamon Bundles

Bundles of cinnamon sticks can be decorated very simply or elaborately, but the key is to choose ribbons which look luxurious and exciting together. We have used two separate colour stories to illustrate the potential. The same decorations can be adapted to gift wrap special presents.

You will need:
1 $^1/_2$in (39mm) wide ribbon in various shades and textures
Assorted narrower ribbons to form roses, ties, bows and trims
Cinnamon sticks
Small dried flowers or leaves in toning shades
Needle and matching thread
All-purpose glue

1 Tie the cinnamon sticks firmly together in bundles of three, using thread to secure.

2 Circle the centre of each bundle with 1 $^1/_2$in (39mm) wide ribbon. Overlap the ends and secure with glue.

3 Decorate each to your liking, with a selection of bows, small ribbon roses, knots, ties and dried flowers.

Bonbonnières

Decoratively packaged sweets for special occasions add an individual touch to any festivity or celebration. They often form an intrinsic part of the table decoration. Using pretty ribbon roses and bows you can create a variety of extravagant confections.

Bonbonnières date back to early European history, when they were given by wealthy aristocrats to celebrate marriages, christenings and birthdays. Originally they were made of gold, precious stones, porcelain or crystal. Even the content was of great value, as sugar was a costly delicacy, prized for its assumed medicinal properties. Almonds have been given at weddings for over a thousand years, but not until the 13th century were they covered with a layer of sugar to become 'confetti'.

Today, the traditional bonbonnière is an exquisite gift containing five almonds, wrapped in layers of lace or net and tied with ribbon, which is often adorned with tiny flowers or pearls. Representing health, wealth, happiness, long life and fertility, the bonbonnière may also be given as a token of thanks, either on its own or to enhance another gift. What better way to celebrate a special occasion, whether it be a wedding, birth, anniversary, graduation or birthday?

These party favours add a very personal touch to a special event and can be as fancy as you wish. Usually three or four layers of tulle are used, often in different shades or textures. The tiny dish, containing the almonds, is placed in the centre of the tulle, which is then drawn up around the dish and tied in a tight knot using a narrow ribbon. The ends of the ribbon are tied into a bow.

As an alternative, miniature baskets or pretty boxes can be filled with confectionery. Ribbon bows and roses are used to decorate the bonbonnière. Stitched roses, made from $^{3}/_{8}$in (9mm) ribbon, or one large rose made from $1^{1}/_{2}$in (39mm) ribbon, make an attractive centrepiece for the tulle bundles or the handles of baskets. Multi-

looped or single bows can be used in abundance. An 18 inch (45cm) length of ribbon will give an attractive single bow with tails, but several ribbons of this length in shaded colours will look more generous. Pre-cut tulles, almonds and dishes are sold specifically for making bonbonnières; enquire at your local craft store.

We have used combinations of ribbon roses, lace, nets, loops and bows to decorate the pretty containers pictured here. Use these ideas and any other trimmings in your handicraft box, to create your own, highly individual bonbonnières.

AB

Ribbon Embroidery

The very word embroidery conjures up peaceful images of Victorian ladies quietly whiling away the hours on tapestry work and samplers. Despite their rather dowdy image, the Victorians were great innovators, finding a variety of ways in which to use ribbons in their embroidery. Very narrow silk ribbons were used instead of threads for canvas work; wider ribbons were used to form flower heads and leaves. This gave their work an attractive three-dimensional effect and introduced subtle changes of colour. Originally the work done by the Victorians was bright and lustrous, but the ribbons were inclined to fade and disintegrate with time.

Today we are able to adapt these traditional techniques, taking full advantage of the ribbons and other embroidery materials available. Properties such as colour fastness and washability are now virtually taken for granted and make ribbon embroidery for soft furnishings and fashion garments a viable proposition.

We are seeing a return to the 'Old World' values, the era of the 'throw-away' society is passing and we are now looking for products that will last, that can be handed down to future generations. The home is once again becoming an important focus; there is a greater emphasis on interior decoration and many traditional crafts are enjoying a renaissance in the 90's.

Embroidery has a wonderful calming effect, a great boon in these pressured, fast-moving times. It is a delightful and relaxing hobby that can be done almost anywhere and is relatively inexpensive. It is enjoying a 'new age' and ribbon is playing a key part in the new movement.

The glorious textures and relative simplicity of ribbon embroidery can be equally enjoyed by complete beginners and the more experienced. If you already embroider, then it is only a matter of experimenting with traditional stitches to see what you can achieve. On the other hand, if embroidery has never tempted you before, then working with ribbon could be just what you have been waiting for!

Combining ribbon with traditional embroidery threads gives scope for all kinds of interesting effects. Couched ribbon makes attractive stems for flowers. Ribbon loops and french knots add dimension and invite an exciting mix of colours. The sheer ribbons give beautiful shadow effects and make gorgeous roses or tulips. If you love canvas work, try ribbons on their own or with tapestry yarns.

The perfectionist should take care to keep the ribbon flat when making a stitch. Those that delight in a celebration of rich and wonderful textural effects can let the ribbon twist, on the basis that it was intended to be that way! Choose the technique that suits your preference. Canvas work requires a flat ribbon stitch everytime; whilst a floral spray, such as the one demonstrated on the picture frame (page 66), is a great project for textural freedom.

Only very basic equipment is needed; needles, scissors and perhaps an embroidery frame are all you need to get started. The stitches used most frequently in ribbonwork are deliberately very simple in order to show the ribbon to best effect. All the projects in this chapter are within the capabilities of the complete beginner. Just a little practice with the basic stitches illustrated on page 62 and you can achieve some very pleasing results. You may even discover a few techniques of your own!

Hints for Ribbon Embroidery

1 The use of an embroidery frame is a purely personal choice, but it often makes the work much easier, especially if you have a tendency to pull the work too tightly. A small frame is all that is required for the projects in this chapter.

2 Try to keep the embroidery fairly loose so that each motif has more texture and emphasizes the three-dimensional effect in the finished project.

3 Never worry about the back of the work. It is far more important to enjoy your stitching and invariably the finished piece will have a backing fabric which will conceal the back.

4 Embroidery is intended to be a relaxing pastime; do not rush it, allow yourself plenty of time to experiment with colour and textural effects that can be created by unusual stitching methods. In short, enjoy it!

5 Work with short lengths of ribbon, 20in (50cm) or less to minimize twisting. If the ribbon does twist, drop the threaded needle and allow it to unwind naturally.

6 To begin embroidery secure the ribbon at the start with a small backstitch.

7 To secure the end of ribbon, weave it behind the stitching or leave a tail of ribbon to be caught by the next stitch. Knotting the ribbon is not recommended as this will create an uneven, bulky finish.

Basic Stitches and Flowers

Backstitch

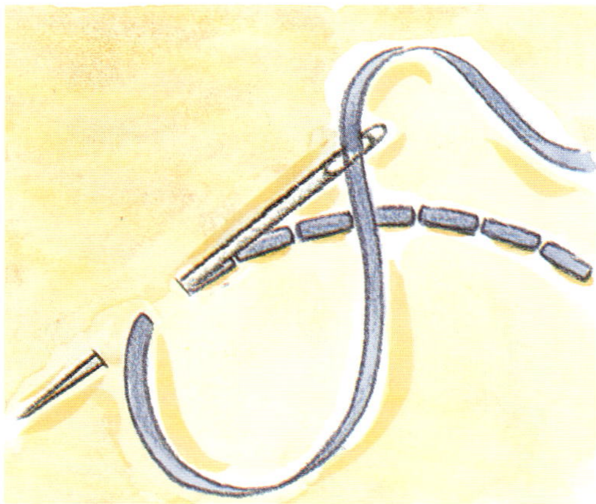

Cross Stitch

Diagonal Stitch

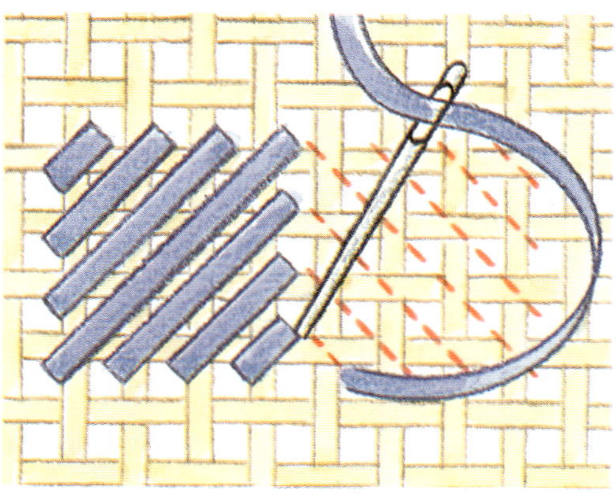

Feather Stitch

1 Bring the ribbon through the fabric at the top point to be worked and make alternate diagonal stitches; first to the left, then to the right. Pull the needle through and over the working ribbon. Graduate the size of the individual stitches so that they resemble a spray of leaves.

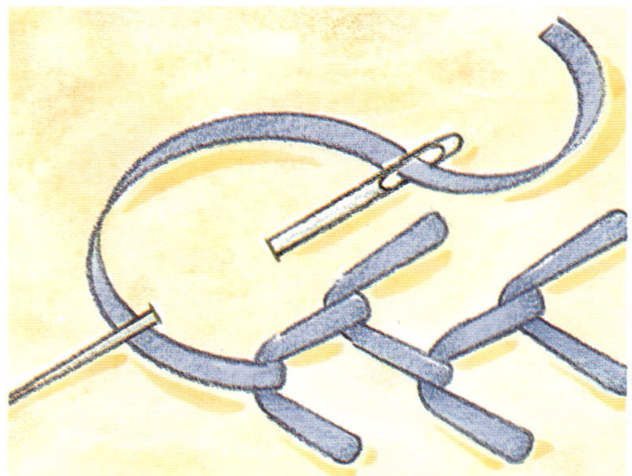

Fly Stitch

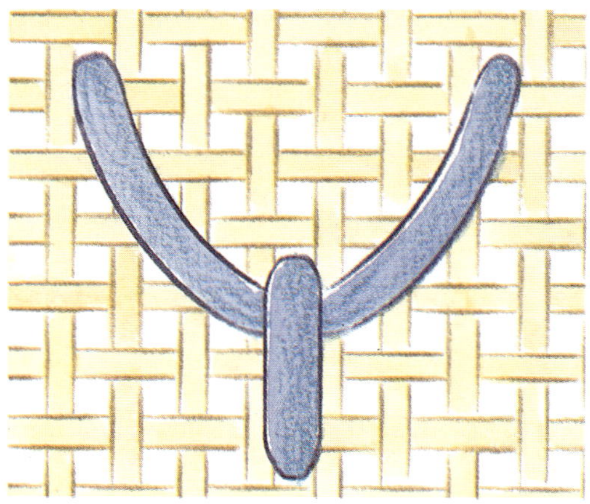

French Knots

1 Bring the ribbon through the fabric to the right side. Hold it taut with the left hand.

2 Twist the needle around the ribbon twice. Still holding the ribbon, neaten the twists then turn the needle and insert it back through the fabric at virtually the same spot where it originally emerged.

3 Pull the needle and ribbon through the twists.

When working with ribbon it is easier to make and finish each knot separately, rather than bringing the needle back through the fabric for the next knot.

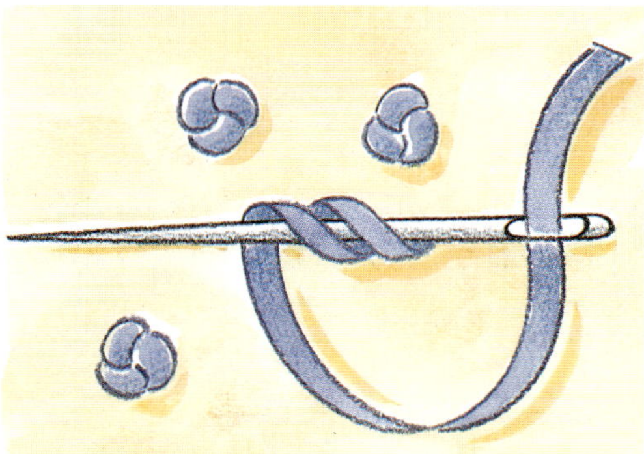

Herringbone Stitch

1 Work from left to right to produce this stitch on two parallel lines.

2 Bring the needle out on the lower line and take it back through on the upper line, a little to the right. Make a small stitch to the left, having the ribbon below the needle.

3 Take the needle back through on the lower line, a little to the right. Make a small stitch to the left, having the ribbon above the needle at this point.

4 Repeat these two movements for the required amount of stitches. The stitches should be evenly spaced for best results.

Loops

Used as a 'filler' stitch on the embroidered picture frame. Simply make small random seed stitches, leaving them loose on the right side of the fabric.

Norwich Stitch

Counting the threads on canvas, bring the needle up on the odd numbers and take it down on the even.

Bring the needle up at 1, count six threads diagonally and go down at 2. Come up at 3 and down at 4. Continue in this pattern. The last stitch worked is 19/20.

Rhodes Stitch
Proceed around the canvas square, following the diagram and ending on a diagonal stitch. Ensure the last stitch worked in each block faces the centre.

Running Stitch

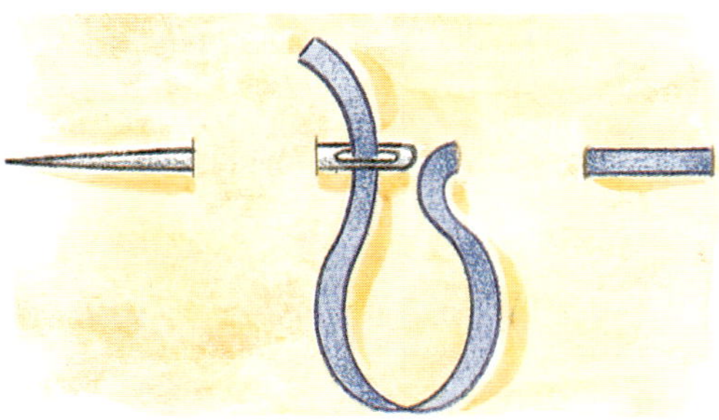

Straight Stitch

Tent Stitch

These illustrations capture the formation of ribbon-embroidered flowers featured in the projects within this chapter. Experiment for varied effects.

Daisies
1 Use a straight stitch to create daisies with five or six petals. Bring the ribbon up at a point equivalent to the outer edge of the flower. Take the ribbon back down through the fabric at the centre of the flower. The first petal has thus been formed.

2 Bring the needle back out again to form the tip of the second petal and take it back down at the flower centre.

3 Continue in this way until all petals are complete.

Detached Chain Stitch/Lazy Daisy Stitch
This stitch can be arranged to look like leaves and buds.

1 Bring the ribbon up through the fabric from the back. Push the needle down again at almost the same point and out again at the required length of the stitch. Catch the loop which is formed and pull.

2 Push the needle in again, over the ribbon loop thus anchoring it in place.

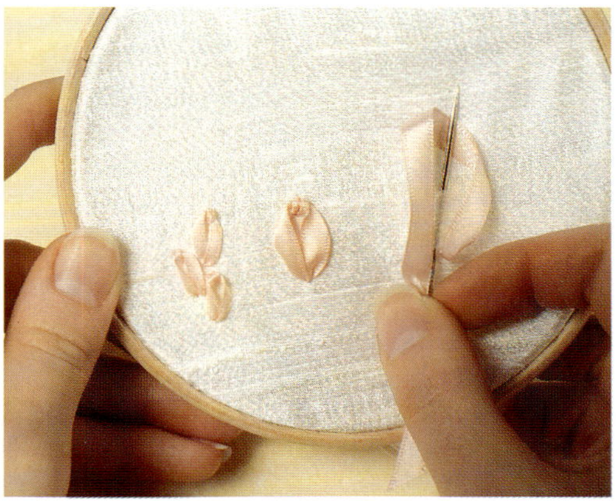

Rosebuds and Tulips
These are created by using two straight stitches. The second stitch starts under the starting point of the first stitch. It finishes over the top of the first stitch finishing point.

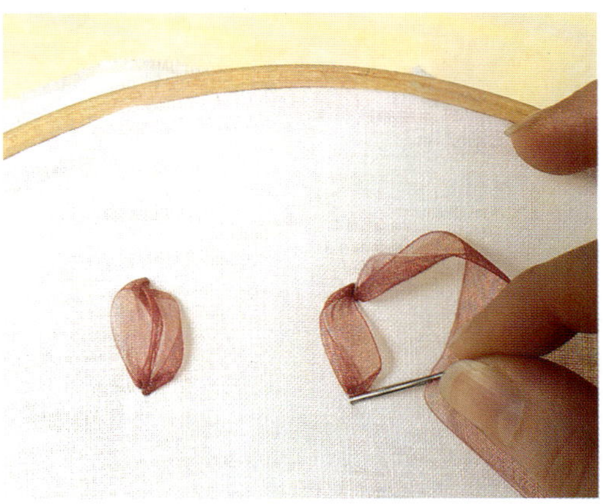

Spider Web Rose
1 Using an embroidery silk, make a five-pronged circle. Anchor the thread securely at the back of the fabric and fasten off. Using a large-eyed, pointed needle, thread the ribbon through from the centre back.

2 Change the needle for a blunt tapestry needle. Weave the ribbon in and out of the prongs in a continuous spiral, until the entire area is filled and the embroidery silk is no longer visible. Do not arrange the ribbon; let it twist in its own natural way.

3 Change back to the pointed tapestry needle to take the ribbon underneath the surface of the rose and back through the fabric near the centre point where it first came through.

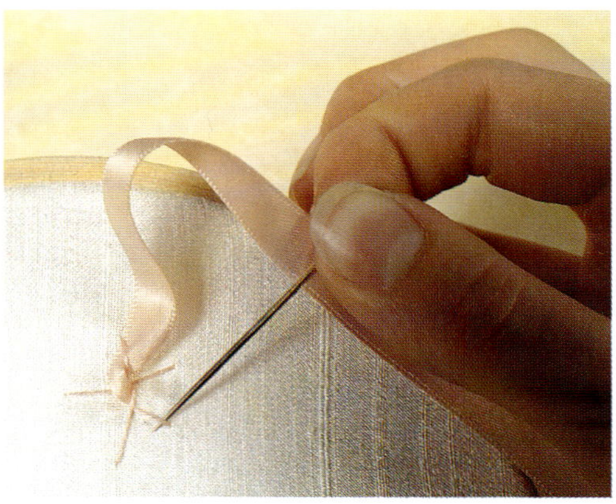

Embroidered Picture Frame

A ribbon embroidered frame gives a romantic aura to a picture that marks a memorable occasion. Silk, pearls and ribbons remaining from a gown will add to the sentimental value.

You will need:
Ivory silk fabric 15x16 $^1/_2$in (38x42cm)
4 $^3/_8$yd (4m) cream sheer ribbon $^1/_2$in (12mm) wide
3 $^1/_4$yd (3m) ivory satin ribbon $^1/_{16}$in (1.5mm) wide
3 $^1/_4$yd (3m) ivory satin ribbon $^1/_8$in (3mm) wide
1 $^1/_8$yd (1m) maize satin ribbon $^1/_8$in (3mm) wide
$^5/_8$yd (50cm) dusty rose satin ribbon $^1/_{16}$in (1.5mm) wide
$^5/_8$yd (50cm) dusty rose satin ribbon $^5/_8$in (15mm) wide
$^5/_8$yd (50cm) cream satin ribbon $^3/_8$in (9mm) wide
$^5/_8$yd (50cm) pale rose satin ribbon $^3/_8$in (9mm) wide
$^5/_8$yd (50cm) tan satin ribbon $^1/_{16}$in (1.5mm) wide
$^5/_8$yd (50cm) maize satin ribbon $^1/_{16}$in (1.5mm) wide
$^5/_8$yd (50cm) white sheer ribbon $^1/_2$in (12mm) wide
Two pieces of mounting board 10x12in (26x30cm)
Cream satin fabric 12x13 $^1/_2$in (30x34cm)
Masking tape
Double-sided tape
Lightweight wadding/batting 10x12in (26x30cm)
Fabric glue
Piece of clear sticky-backed plastic 7x5 $^1/_2$in (18x14cm)
4 small pearl beads

Key to Stitches

1 Detached chain stitch: ivory satin $^1/_{16}$in (1.5mm)
2 French knots: dusty rose satin $^1/_{16}$in (1.5mm)
3 Detached chain stitch: ivory satin $^1/_8$in (3mm)
4 French knots: white sheer $^1/_2$in (12mm)
5 Daisies: maize satin $^1/_{16}$in (1.5mm)
6 Rose No 2: cream sheer $^1/_2$in (12mm)
7 Rose No 6: dusty rose satin $^5/_8$in (15mm)
8 Rose No 3: cream satin $^3/_8$in (9mm)
9 Rose No 1: cream sheer $^1/_2$in (12mm)
10 Loops: maize and ivory satin $^1/_8$in (3mm)
11 Rose No 4: cream sheer $^1/_2$in (12mm)
12 Rose No 5: pale rose satin $^3/_8$in (9mm)
13 Detached chain stitch: ivory satin $^1/_8$in (3mm)
14 Bow: cream sheer $^1/_2$in (12mm) and ivory satin $^1/_{16}$in (1.5mm)
15 Feather stitch: maize satin $^1/_8$in (3mm)
16 French knots: tan satin $^1/_{16}$in (1.5mm)
17 Straight stitch: ivory satin $^1/_{16}$in (1.5mm)

A tapestry needle with a blunt point to weave the ribbon for the Spider Web Rose technique.

One, possibly two large-eyed, sharp point tapestry needles which will be used to pull the ribbon through the fabric. It is important to use a large-eyed tapestry needle as it will separate rather than break the fabric threads, and allow the ribbon to pass through. Two needles may be required to accommodate the varying ribbon widths.

Embroidery

1 Outline the shape of the frame in running stitch.

2 Following the chart start with Rose No 1, using the Spider Web technique (detailed in Basic Stitches earlier). Continue in sequence until all six roses are completed.

3 Embroider maize and ivory-coloured loops between the roses using the 1/8in (3mm) ribbon. Work detached chain stitch to form leaves outside the roses. Embroider the tall leaves at the top of the picture using detached chain stitch and french knots. Add the straight stitch daisies and flower stems. Complete all other embroidery work following the chart. Make up the cream and ivory single loop bow and stitch in place using sewing thread.

4 The single rose in the bottom right hand corner is woven in the same way as the others, except two ribbons are threaded through the needle and woven together. Work two rosebuds as shown on page 65.

Picture Frame

1 Cut the aperture in one piece of mounting board (6 1/4x4 3/4in / 16x12cm). Cut the wadding to match and lay it on this mounting board.

2 Stretch the embroidered silk over the board and secure neatly with masking tape at the back. Ensure the running stitch outline reaches the edges of the board. Carefully make a vertical cut in the middle of the silk. Now cut to each corner of the aperture. Fold the silk to the back and fix with masking tape. A tiny spot of glue in each corner will prevent the fabric from fraying. Place a small pearl bead at each corner to cover any raw edges.

3 Cover the second piece of mounting board with the cream satin fabric in the same way but do not, of course, cut an aperture in this board. Place the sticky-backed plastic on the wrong side of this board to give a smooth finish. With wrong sides together, stick the back to the front using double-sided tape on three sides only. Leave the top edge or one side open to insert the photograph.

Finished frame size 10x12in (26x30cm)
Aperture size 6 1/4 x4 3/4 in (16x12cm)

Ribbon Embroidery Sampler

Samplers go back to the 16th Century when they were originally 'needlework notes' worked on a piece of linen and kept in the workbox as a reference. By the time the Victorians were stitching their samplers they had become an intriguing mix of motifs which often illustrated the life of the stitcher.

Using a collection of basic stitches and techniques, our sampler explores some of the many possibilities for ribbon embroidery. It is a good starting point for those embarking on ribbon embroidery for the first time. You could add important dates and initials that are significant to you. The colours chosen are in a natural, country style. It is possible to create a very different look, using pretty pastels for a lighter, more contemporary setting. Once you have grasped the basics, you can create your own symbolic designs in ribboncraft.

You will need:
$^1/_8$in (3mm) wide doubleface satin ribbon in the following quantities and colours:
4 $^3/_8$yd (4m) light navy
3 $^1/_4$yd (3m) forest green
5 $^1/_2$yd (5m) scarlet
3 $^1/_4$yd (3m) wine red
1 $^5/_8$yd (1.5m) smoke blue
1 $^5/_8$yd (1.5m) soft jade
4 $^3/_8$yd (4m) sand dune

Heavy-weight card 8 $^3/_4$x12in (22x30cm)
28 count embroidery linen 12 $^1/_4$x15 $^3/_4$in (31x40cm)
Sewing thread
Buttonhole thread
Red embroidery thread
Fusible interfacing 4in (10cm) square
Tapestry needle with blunt point
Frame 8 $^3/_4$x12in (22x30cm)
Sharp sewing needle, pins and iron
Workboard

1 Neaten the edges of the fabric by turning under a small hem. Fold the fabric in half both ways and mark the centre with a line of tacking.

2 Count 126 threads out from the centre to each side. Tack a vertical line to mark the sides of the sampler. Count 172 threads up and down from the centre to mark the top and bottom edges of the sampler in the same way. You should have a 2in (5cm) margin all the way round the fabric.

3 Cut twenty pieces each of the wine red and sand dune ribbons, each 4in (10cm) long. Plain weave a square onto the interfacing, using the wine ribbon vertically and the sand dune horizontally. Leave a margin of just under $^5/_8$in (15mm) all the way round. Follow the technique instructions for plain weaving on page 28.

4 Using the template, cut a heart shape from the woven square. Lay the point of the heart to the edge of the woven square and cut out, adding a $^5/_8$in (15mm) turning allowance around the curved edges.

5 Fold and tack the allowance under, clipping the curves to allow for ease. Tack the heart in position, centrally on the embroidery linen. Work french knots around it in forest green, scarlet and jade.

6 Embroider the border as shown. Make a running stitch in red embroidery thread. Weave light navy and scarlet ribbon through the running stitches.

7 To mount the completed sampler, align the

Key to Stitches
□ = 2 threads × 2 threads

Top Panel:
Alphabet: Backstitch
Flowers: French knots, detached chain stitch
Daffodils: Fly stitch with two straight stitches
Line: Herringbone

Lower Panel:
Bows: Chain stitch, straight stitch
People: Fly stitch, french knots, straight stitch
Line: Herringbone

Border:
Red running stitch interlaced with light navy and scarlet ribbons

ABC 123

heavy-weight card with the tacked perimeter lines on the linen. Fold the allowances to the back of the card. Thread a needle with buttonhole thread and, starting from the centre, lace back and forth from top to bottom of the sampler back, then from side to side, pulling the linen tight as you go. The sampler is now ready for framing.

Scale: 1 square = $^1/_2$ in (12 mm)

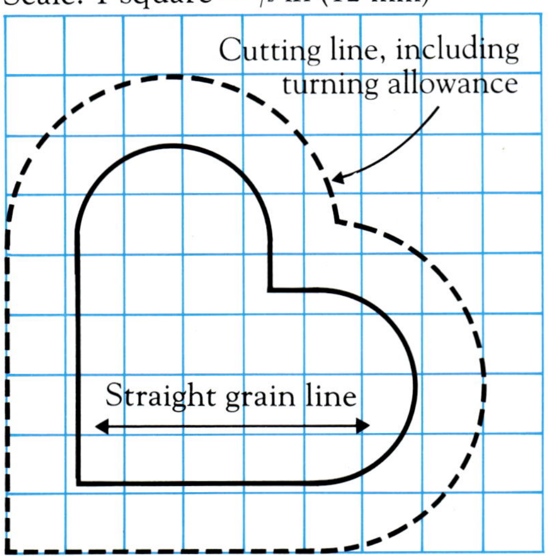

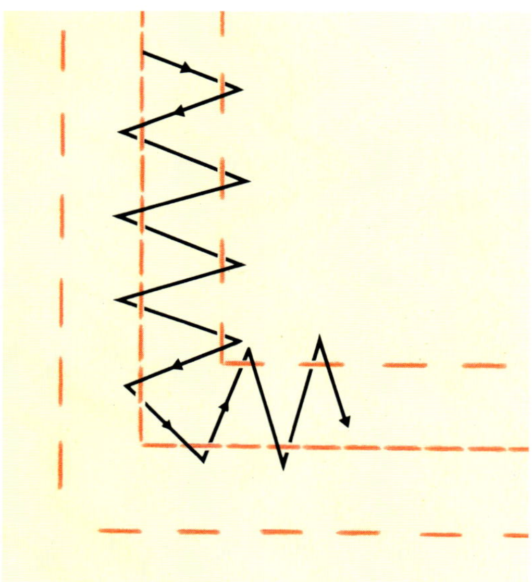

NEEDLECASE

Canvas embroidery takes on a new dimension when worked entirely or partially in ribbon. You can use $^1/_{16}$in or $^1/_8$in (1.5mm or 3mm) ribbon on its own, or in conjunction with embroidery or tapestry yarns. Take care to ensure that the ribbon remains flat when each stitch is formed.

All ribbons used for this needlecase are doubleface satin, $^1/_{16}$in (1.5mm) wide.

Ribbons you will need:
1 $^1/_8$yd (1m) pale yellow
2 $^1/_4$yd (2m) white
3 $^1/_4$yd (3m) pale blue
2 $^3/_4$yd (2.5m) mid blue
4 $^3/_8$yd (4m) yellow
9 $^1/_4$yd (8.5m) deep blue

10-hole canvas 4 $^3/_8$x7in (11x18cm)
Lining fabric 4 $^3/_8$x7in (11x18cm)
Felt 2 $^3/_4$x5 $^1/_2$in (7x14cm)
Scissors
Large-eyed tapestry needle
Sewing thread

Note: The chart represents half of the design.

1 Complete the embroidery, following the chart and working down the canvas. Starting with the deep blue ribbon, count five holes down and five holes in from the short side of the canvas. Work diagonal stitches.

2 Finish the embroidery with a tent stitch border, using the deep blue ribbon; this is not shown on the chart. The stitches will cover one thread only.

3 Trim the canvas to within three threads of the embroidery. Fold a narrow hem to the wrong side, all the way round the canvas.

4 To make the needlecase loop and tie use excess ribbon pieces. First bring three ribbons (about 3in/7.5cm long) through the canvas at the point (•) marked on the chart. Take them through to the back, leaving a small loop on the right side. Fasten off securely.

5 At the opposite end of the case, attach five ribbons at the wrong side and bring them through to the front. Trim the ribbons to about 6in (15cm). Make a knot one third of the way down the length.

6 Press a hem on all four edges of the lining. With wrong sides facing, slipstitch the lining to the needlecase. Trim the felt to size and place in the centre of the lining. Stitch through all three layers, down the middle of the case. Fold the completed case in half.

CHART KEY
Rhodes stitch - pale blue
Cross stitch - white
Diagonal stitch – yellow
Diagonal stitch – mid blue
Diagonal stitch – deep blue
Norwich stitch – pale yellow
Tent stitch – deep blue

Rosettes, Braids and Tassels

I always remember my grandmother's sewing basket with a smile and a little nostalgia; the joy of idly stirring the contents of the button compartment, and the discovery of a long forgotten, decorative rosette among the delightful mélange of hatpins, threads and braids.

Since the dawn of civilization, man has added decoration to both the grandest and most humble of his possessions. Consequently, there is a great deal documented on the subject. Up until the earlier part of this century, ribbon was widely used for millinery and rosettes were an artform with almost limitless scope for invention.

The Victorians loved these wonderful embellishments and invented literally hundreds of variations for soft furnishings and garment decoration. The rich colours and substantial fabrics of that era lent themselves beautifully to such adornments. During the 1920's and 30's they enjoyed a revival and now, several decades later, we are experiencing an upsurge of interest once again.

Tassels have existed in one form or another for centuries. Their original function was to hold threads together in a tidy bunch, however they soon became a decorative trim in their own right and different styles rapidly developed. Making a basic tassel with $^1/_{16}$in (1.5mm) ribbon is easy. The addition of fine gold thread gives a more opulent look, while the tassel top can be as elaborate as you wish.

Rosettes, braids and tassels provide that certain flair and elegance. They exist solely to embellish and adorn anything and everything in soft furnishings, garments and fashion accessories. They can vary in complexity according to the crafter's skill and taste, although it is often the simplest designs that look stunning, showing off the ribbon to best effect. They are all fun to make and varying ribbon widths allow you to carry over the theme of colour and texture which you may have used in a larger ribbon project. For example, a woven or appliquéd cushion, made in a $^7/_8$in (23mm) turquoise satin ribbon, can have a plait around its border and a tassel at each corner crafted from the same colourway in a $^1/_{16}$in (1.5mm) width.

The following chapter illustrates the basics of ribbon folding, pleating, plaiting and gathering. After completing a basic rosette you will realize the endless possibilities for expanding the designs and combining your own ideas. Creating these wonderful adornments is incredibly satisfying and they add a beautiful finish to both handcrafted and ready-made items that need a personal touch. Making rosettes is a very adaptable artform and old techniques have been given a new twist to make them appropriate for today's style.

Rosettes are made from ribbon that is cut or folded in various ways to give an attractive shape. The folding is simple. Short ribbon pieces are often just halved in the middle, or longer lengths may be knife-pleated or gathered.

The beauty of the rosette lies in the layout of these folded, pleated or gathered ribbons. Usually they are stitched, in circles, semi-circles or spirals, to a base of substantial canvas or interfacing. The rosette can be composed of a mixture of ribbon treatments. For example, a pleated ribbon might form the outside of the rosette. In the layer below you could place a row of folded ribbons, followed by a row of pointed petals.

Pointed petals are made by folding the ribbon at the centre point and bringing the ends to cross at the centre and then away at opposite angles. The photographed steps show how easily the ribbons are transformed into interesting shapes.

The design possibilities are numerous and you can have fun creating some interesting combinations. The centre of the rosette is often finished with a covered button, tassel or ribbon rose. As with most ribbon adornments, the finished size of a rosette will depend upon the width of the ribbons used, and also how closely they are layered. Start with a simple design using plains, plaids or prints and then go on to invent your own combinations.

Braids and tassels can be used instead of rosettes, or as part of a rosette decoration. Unlike a straight ribbon, a plaited braid can go around curves and makes for an unusual edging for both home and fashion accessories.

Flat plaits, using three or five strands of narrow ribbon, are best made in $^{1}/_{16}$ to $^{1}/_{8}$in (1.5 to 3mm) ribbon widths. Loop braids however, can be made successfully with ribbons up to $^{1}/_{2}$ in (12mm) wide, which will give quite a wide finished trim.

When complete, a light press with a moderate iron will set the braid and reduce ribbon movement that could distort the finished braid.

ROSETTES

Here, an attractive collection of ribbon rosettes has been used to embellish silk purses. The same rosettes could be used to decorate hats, picture bows, soft furnishings or garments. They are equally eye-catching placed in the centre of bows for the Christmas tree and garlands, or for decorative gift packaging.

The canvas circle size for any rosette will be determined by the width of ribbon used and the required size of the finished rosette. Most are between 1 and 2 $^1/_2$in (2.5 and 6.25cm) in diameter. As a rough guide, most rosettes will generally require a total of 1 $^1/_8$ to 2 $^3/_4$yd (1 to 2.5m).

Catherine Wheel Rosettes

Suitable ribbon widths: 1 $^1/_8$yd (1m) of $^5/_8$in, $^7/_8$in or 1 $^1/_2$in (15mm, 23mm or 39mm) wide ribbon.

1 Cut a circle of canvas approximately 1 $^1/_2$in (4cm) in diameter. Cut the circle smaller for the $^5/_8$in (15mm) ribbon and slightly larger for the 1 $^1/_2$in (39mm) ribbon. Cut fourteen pieces of ribbon, each 2in (5cm) long. Fold each piece in half along the width of the ribbon and press. Position these 'petals' around the canvas circle, overlapping each piece to form a spiral effect.

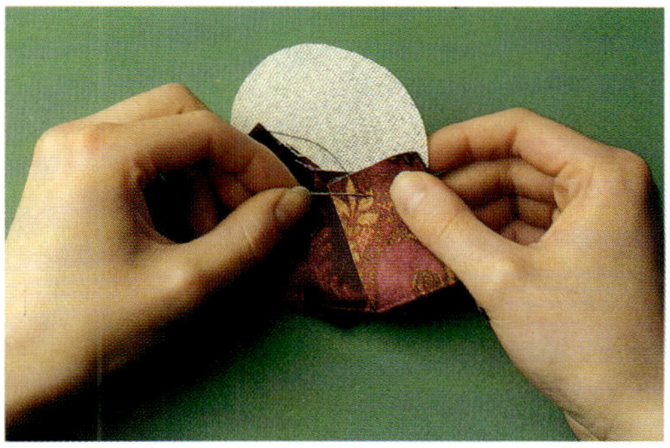

2 Stitch in place. Finish the centre with a covered button or a ribbon rose as illustrated here. This rosette is featured on the Regency Barrel Cushion (page 97) and is a good example of the effect that can be achieved by combining different ribboncraft techniques within the same project.

Leaf Point Rosettes

Interesting effects can be achieved using the following folding technique.

Suitable ribbon widths: $^7/_8$in or 1 $^1/_2$in (23mm or 39mm).

1 Cut the ribbon into 3 or 3 $^1/_2$in (7.5 or 8.75cm) lengths. Fold each piece in half, as for the Catherine Wheel.

2 Fold the top corners down, forming a point. Stitch the corners where they meet.

Petal Point Rosettes

Suitable ribbon widths: $^1/_2$in, $^5/_8$in and $^7/_8$in (12mm, 15mm and 23mm).

1 Cut the ribbon into strips approximately 3 $^3/_4$in (9.5cm) long if using $^7/_8$in (23mm) ribbon width; 3in (7.5cm) strips for $^1/_2$in and $^5/_8$in (12mm and 15mm) widths.

2 Cross the ribbon, pressing it flat at the centre to form a point. Make a neat stitch to hold it in place.

3 Position on the circle of canvas backing fabric and stitch to secure. Work as many petal points as necessary to complete the circle.

Pleated Rosettes

Suitable ribbon widths: $^7/_8$in and 1 $^1/_2$in (23mm or 39mm).

1 Pleat the ribbon and stitch along one edge to secure as shown.

You can create a variety of effects by applying pleated ribbon to form a circle or crescent-shape on the backing canvas. To calculate the amount of ribbon required, simply multiply the finished pleat length by three.

Plaiting

As already demonstrated in previous pages, many interesting effects can be achieved by folding and pleating ribbons to produce luxurious rosettes and unusual trims. Using ribbons of narrower widths, beautiful plaits and braids can be worked to create decorative edgings for all manner of applications. Always press the finished work to set the ribbon.

3-Strand Plait

A basic 3-strand plait is worked in $^{1}/_{16}$in (1.5mm) or $^{1}/_{8}$in (3mm) satin ribbon. 12in (30cm) ribbon lengths will give a 9in (22.5cm) plait, approximately.

1 Pin three strands together on a pinboard. Plait in the usual way, keeping the right side of the ribbon facing towards you throughout.

2 Finish with a knot or stitch to secure at both ends. Press with a moderate, dry iron.

The 3-strand plait makes a perfect edging for both weaving and appliqué projects; it is especially useful along curved edges.

5-Strand Plait

Using five strands of $^{1}/_{16}$in (1.5mm) or $^{1}/_{8}$in (3mm) satin ribbon, a very attractive braid can be created. 12in (30cm) ribbon lengths will create an 8in (20cm) plait, approximately.

1 Pin five lengths of ribbon side by side on a pinboard. Working from one edge, bring the outside strand to the centre, taking it under the adjacent strand, over the next, under and over to the end. Repeat until the braid is complete.

2 Secure both ends with a few hand stitches. Press lightly with a moderate, dry iron to 'set' the braid.

Slip Knot Braid

Use $^{1}/_{16}$in, $^{1}/_{8}$in, $^{3}/_{8}$in or $^{5}/_{8}$in (1.5mm, 3mm, 9mm or 15mm) ribbon for this plaiting technique. You will need to multiply the required finished length by nine to obtain the approximate amount of ribbon required.

1 Form a loop at the ends of two ribbons of the same width. Pass one ribbon loop through the other and stitch to secure.

2 Make another loop and insert this through the existing loop. Pull lightly before forming another loop and repeat the process.

3 Continue working loops, alternating the insertion of one inside the other. Pull lightly after each insertion to maintain an even tension along the braid as you work.

4 Neaten the ends to finish.

Ribbon Tassels

To make one 2 $^{3}/_{4}$in (7cm) tassel you will need:
2yd (1.80m) doubleface satin ribbon $^{1}/_{16}$in (1.5mm) wide
1 $^{3}/_{4}$yd (1.60m) gold lurex sewing thread (optional)
Piece of card 2 $^{3}/_{4}$x4in (7x10cm)
Needle and matching thread or all-purpose glue

1 Cut one ribbon length of 6 $^{1}/_{4}$in (16cm) and a second length of 4in (10cm). Wind the remaining ribbon around the narrow width of the card, making sure that it is laid evenly. Thread the 6 $^{1}/_{4}$in (16cm) length of ribbon under the wound ribbon. Pull it to the edge of the card and knot it firmly, leaving two equal tails for attachment to your project. Slide the ribbon off the card.

2 Hold the ribbon firmly by the attaching tails and wind the remaining piece of ribbon around the looped strands to form the tassel neck. Secure the ends as invisibly as possible, with either glue or thread.

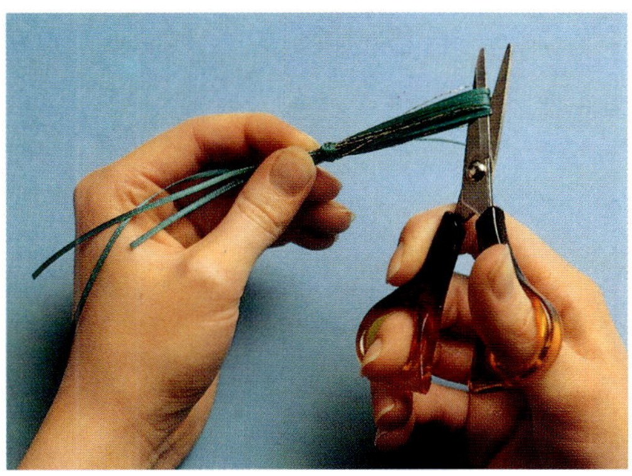

3 Cut through the ribbon loops and trim the tassel end. If using the gold thread, wind it simultaneously with the ribbon for added effect. Use tassels on soft furnishings, clothing and even gift packaging.

Plaid Christmas Baubles

The idea of the traditional Christmas, dominated by a magnificent fir tree laden with decorations and lights, was a charming custom brought to England from Germany by Queen Victoria's beloved consort, Prince Albert.

Trimming the tree is a ritual in which everyone likes to have a share and handmade ornaments give a highly personal touch. There are many ways to decorate baubles with ribbon, most of which are deceptively easy. A simple folding technique turns traditional plaids in festive reds and greens into beautiful adornments for the Christmas tree. Choose your own combination of ribbons; red satin ribbon with gold and grosgrain go well together.

Ring the seasonal changes in your home decor by varying the ribbon to give interesting colour and pattern combinations; welcome Easter and the Spring using ribbon in canary yellow and dew-fresh green. Different polystyrene shapes and sizes make for an interesting collection; a focal point in any room or hallway.

For each bauble you will need:
Colour No 1: 1 $^5/_8$yd (1.50m) of 2 $^1/_4$in (56mm) wide ribbon
Colour No 2: 1 $^5/_8$yd (1.50m) of 1 $^1/_2$in (39mm) wide ribbon
$^5/_8$yd (50cm) red satin ribbon $^1/_8$in (3mm) wide
One red ribbon rose
One polystyrene 3in (7.5cm) goose egg
140 plain sharp pins

I recommend the use of a thimble when making any baubles which require pin work.

1 Measure and cut ribbon No 1 and 2 into squares.

2 Place one square of No 1 over the centre of the narrow end of the egg and pin the four corners in place. Place a pin in the middle, which will later be removed. This will aid alignment of the triangles.

3 Take all the ribbon squares and fold diagonally to form a triangle. Fold diagonally again. Press the creases well as you do this. If using a patterned ribbon, you should now choose the side of the triangle which you wish to use.

4 Starting at the narrow end, place four triangles of No 1 around the egg, having the point of the triangle facing towards the pin in the middle of the square. Pin the bottom corners of the triangle to the egg.

5 Now add four triangles of No 2 and place these around the egg in between the other triangles. Keep the base lines as even as possible. Four plain and four patterned triangles form one round. Start the next round of triangles $^{3}/_{16}$in (5mm) down from the previous layer. Always ensure that the pins in the previous row are hidden by each successive row.

Keeping the pattern straight, continue until the entire egg is covered.

6 Cover the rounded bottom end of the egg with a square of ribbon. Turn under the raw edges of the square and conceal the pins in this hem. Finish the plaid bauble with a hanging loop of $^{1}/_{8}$in (3mm) wide satin ribbon and a ribbon rose.

Note: Decorative baubles can also be made from polystyrene balls or smaller egg shapes. Adjust the ribbon widths to suit.

Country Découpage Hat Box

Découpage was first heard of in the 12th Century and was reputed to have been a European folk art. It reached a much wider audience in 17th Century Venice where it was used to embellish painted furniture. Venetian craftsmen used découpage, with great success, to imitate lacquered furniture.

The craftsmen would create and colour their own designs before cutting them out and pasting them onto furniture. The furniture was then lacquered repeatedly until the images appeared to sink into the wood and look as though they were hand painted. By the 18th Century this Venetian craft had spread to France and it was here that the word découpage was coined; from the French verb, découper, which means 'to cut'.

It is this traditional art form that inspired ribbon découpage which, in turn, gave a new textural effect to the craft. The cut-edge craft ribbons are well suited to this technique, allowing you to cut shapes without fear of the ribbon fraying. The craft ribbon can also be folded along its length and a row of uniform, simple shapes can be cut. In addition to providing an interesting surface texture, découpage in craft ribbons also offers the opportunity to co-ordinate the project with ribbon roses and bows of matching ribbon; a distinct advantage over paper découpage.

Using ribbon découpage in country checks and floral prints, as we have for the hat box, you can create a wonderful patchwork effect in a fraction of the time taken for the more traditional hand sewn variety. The lid of the hat box is a particularly good example of this effect.

You will need:
1 $^{3}/_{8}$yd (1.20m) blue gingham ribbon
6in (15cm) red gingham ribbon
6in (15cm) green gingham ribbon
1 $^{1}/_{8}$yd (1m) blue floral ribbon
6in (15cm) green floral ribbon
6in (15cm) bordeaux floral ribbon
16in (40cm) rose chintz ribbon
28in (70cm) bordeaux gingham ribbon
2 $^{5}/_{8}$in (67mm) wide
1 $^{1}/_{8}$yd (1m) plain bordeaux ribbon
2 $^{7}/_{8}$in (72mm) wide

With the exception of two ribbons, all other craft ribbons used for this hat box are 2in (50mm) wide.

Plain, purchased hat box, approximately 12 $^{3}/_{4}$in (32cm) diameter, 39in (98cm) circumference, 8 $^{1}/_{4}$in (21cm) high
Glue
Clear varnish
Fine sandpaper
Two sheets brown paper 20x28in (50x70cm)
Scissors
Ruler
Pencil
Paint
Paint Brush for varnish and paint
Card and tracing paper

1 Prepare the hat box by painting the interior surfaces with the colour of your choice.

2 Using glue, cover the exterior surfaces with brown paper. Use the lid and the box base as templates to cut two circles from the paper, adding a $^{5}/_{8}$in (15mm) turning allowance all the way round. Clip the allowances on the base circle. Place the box on top of the circle then glue the allowance up to the box sides. Repeat this step with the box lid.

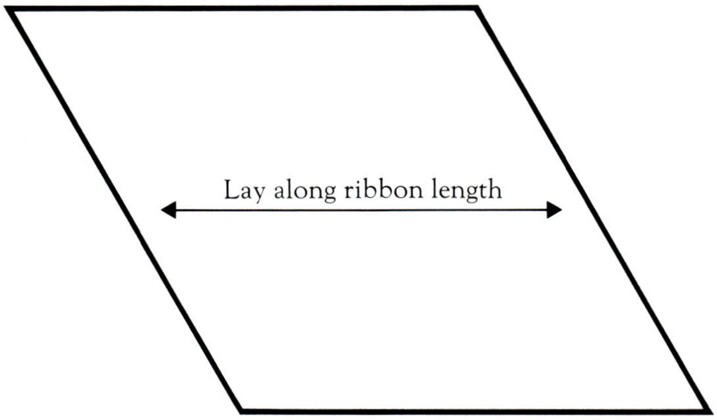

3 Trim the lid edge with the 2in (50mm) wide, blue gingham ribbon, overlapping the ends by about $^3/_8$in (9mm). Glue in place.

4 Cover the box sides with brown paper, taking the paper to the upper and lower edges only, do not add a turning allowance.

5 Trace the diamond shape shown and make a template using the card. Cut the following diamond shapes from 2in (50mm) wide ribbon: six in chintz and two each in blue gingham, red gingham, green gingham, blue floral, green floral and bordeaux floral.

6 Mark the centre of the box lid. Work the patchwork design, using the photograph for guidance, and glue the diamonds in place. To ensure greater accuracy in laying down the patchwork, mark guidelines lightly in pencil. The ribbon will cover the pencil lines.

7 Now take the box and mark a line around the box which is 1 $^1/_2$in (4cm) from the bottom. Use this line for guidance as you glue the plain bordeaux ribbon in place around the box. Overlap the ends slightly.

8 To create the hearts we have to make a ribbon chain. Fold the bordeaux gingham ribbon in a concertina fashion, creating nine layers, each measuring approximately 2 $^7/_8$in (72mm). Trace the heart-shape template and place it on top of the layers. Cut the heart-shape through all layers, but do not cut at points X and Y. Open out the hearts and cut the chain into three strings, each having three hearts. Put to one side.

9 Trace the bow shapes given and cut three sets of these templates from the remaining blue floral ribbon.

10 Glue the heart chains onto the bordeaux ribbon around the hat box. Place in the middle of the ribbon, leaving about 4 $^{1}/_{2}$in (11cm) between each set of three. Position and glue the bow pieces in the spaces remaining.

11 To complete the découpage, varnish the entire box several times. The number of coats will depend on the finished look you wish to achieve. This hat box was varnished seven times, and carefully sanded before the final coat.

Regency Barrel Cushion

The exuberance of Regency, with its exotic oriental and Indian influences, inspired these cushions. The deep colours of tapestries and old leather found in dark, panelled drawing rooms and libraries have a timelessness that complement many home settings today.

Interesting prints and toning plain satin ribbons are appliquéd, woven, plaited or made into rosettes to form an eye-catching group of cushions that would be equally well placed on an antique sofa, an ultra-modern chair or in the comfort of a conservatory. A rich shot silk has been used as the background fabric, adding the exclusive appeal of this designer collection.

For the bolster cushion you will need:
1 $^3/_8$yd (1.30m) plain gold satin ribbon $^7/_8$in (23mm) wide
5 $^3/_4$yd (5.20m) printed satin ribbon $^7/_8$in (23mm) wide
8 $^3/_4$yd (8m) plain gold satin ribbon $^1/_8$in (3mm) wide
1 $^1/_8$yd (1m) silk 45in (115cm) wide
1 $^3/_8$yd (1.30m) piping cord
16in (40cm) zip
Barrel cushion pad 18in (45cm) long, 8in (20cm) in diameter

Note: A seam allowance of $^5/_8$in (15mm) has been included on all fabric requirements.

1 Cut a rectangle of silk 19 $^1/_4$x26 $^1/_4$in (48x65.5cm) and two circles, each 9 $^1/_4$in (23cm) in diameter, to cover the cushion pad.

2 To mark the ribbon positions fold vertical lines on the silk rectangle and press lightly with a moderate iron. These crease lines will act as a stitching guideline. Pin or lightly glue (with fabric glue stick) the printed ribbon and the narrow plain ribbon in place. Machine, sewing both edges in the same direction to prevent any puckering.

3 Cut the remaining $^1/_8$in (3mm) ribbon into three equal lengths and plait them (refer to page 83). Press. Place the plait in the centre of each printed ribbon and machine.

4 With right sides together you can now machine the cushion cover together joining the short edges. Ensure that the ribbons match up at the seam and leave sufficient opening for the zip. Machine or hand stitch the zip in place.

5 Cut two lengths of piping cord to go around each end of the bolster. Cut bias strips of silk (1 $^1/_4$in/3cm wide) to cover the cord, joining the strips where necessary. Encase the piping cord and tack the raw edges together. Carefully interweave the cord ends before covering with the bias strip, ensuring a firm, continuous circle of piping.

6 To ease the piping cord around the circular shape, cut notches along the raw edge before tacking it to the right side of the bolster ends. Do not clip right up to the seamline. The piping cord should lie next to the stitching line. Machine the piped circular ends to the barrel cushion, right sides together.

Clip to ease, turn to right side and press.

Appliqué and Ribbon Patchwork

The basic techniques for ribbon appliqué are few, but if you follow them you can enjoy spectacular results. Almost any woven ribbon can be used to produce attractive items with which to personalize soft furnishings, garments and gifts. Ribbon appliqué offers the perfect opportunity to co-ordinate colour schemes and produce a designer touch.

The scale of most designs can be adjusted by increasing or decreasing the number or widths of ribbons used.

Non-woven interfacing and fusing webs are useful aids in stabilizing and securing ribbons to give a professional finish. A lightweight iron-on quality can be fused to the wrong side of fabric which is to be appliquéd to give extra substance and stability to the weave. This will help eliminate distortion when the ribbon is applied.

For the same reasons, a sew-in interfacing of medium weight will make a good foundation for projects that require total coverage with ribbon, such as the Teddy's Waistcoat (page 102) and the Cot Cover (page 108). Both are backed with another fabric to conceal the interfacing.

A fusible web applied to the wrong side of the ribbon and then ironed onto the fabric will serve a dual purpose. Not only will it stabilize the ribbon, giving it a slightly firmer handle, it also saves pinning and tacking.

The additional guidelines below will help you to achieve the best results with your appliqué projects:

If you are going to trim a garment, always make sure it is shrink resistant and colourfast before you start.

It is worthwhile planning your design on paper to ensure accurate calculations for ribbon quantities and widths. Add extra for joining or neatening ends and for seam allowances.

Draw the design lines on the garment or project using a vanishing marker pen or dressmaker's chalk. If appropriate, a pressed creaseline is a very easy, simple way to mark the ribbon position.

Pinning and tacking ribbon in place for appliqué can be time consuming; care must be taken to ensure the weave does not get damaged or distorted. For ease and speed, you could use a light application of fabric glue or fusible hemming web.

It is easier to apply ribbon to a flat item, that is, before it is made up. However, if trimming something like the purchased pillowcase (page 114), you can make a neater job by opening up the seams a little to conceal the ribbon ends in the seam allowance.

The golden rule when machining ribbon is always to machine both edges in the same direction, otherwise you will see puckering.

Twin needle attachments are marvellous for sewing both edges of narrow ribbons at the same time; what a time saver!

Polyester thread is recommended for machine stitching; if the ribbon does pucker, try a larger stitch or loosen the top tension.

When working with velvet ribbon, avoid crushing the fabric pile by using a zipper foot attachment.

Use a tiny hem stitch for hand sewn appliqué.

CO-ORDINATED CUSHION COLLECTION

Choose a colour theme or a co-ordinated collection of ribbon prints and appliqué them to a complimentary background fabric. By changing the layout of the ribbons on the fabric, or the cushion shape and size, each one will look a little different.

Press a crease in the fabric to give an accurate guide for placing the edge of the ribbon before machining. This will save considerable time by eliminating the need for pinning and tacking. The ribbons are placed in position and machined one at a time, thus creating a woven effect where they cross at each corner. If you prefer to secure the ribbon in some way before stitching, a very narrow strip of fusible webbing, or a light application of fabric glue stick will do the job well.

The Love Knot Cushion adds dimension to the collection and is created from one bias-cut strip of the cushion fabric. This is ribbon appliquéd before backing with a co-ordinating fabric, then attached to the diagonally opposite corners of the cushion. A simple, yet very stylish knot supplies the finishing touch.

Reflect the colours of the ribbons by

Note: A $^{5}/_{8}$in (15mm) seam allowance has been included on all fabric requirements.

using two complimentary colours, one for the top of the cushion and one for the underside and piped edging. The crushed raspberry tone of the silk reflects the colour in this ribbon design.

Enjoy picking colours to match a favourite chair, sofa or bedspread. For a children's nursery experiment with primary brights or novelty prints. For a kitchen or conservatory select fresh greens, yellows and blues in checks and stripes; or enjoy the zany paintbox brights. The joy of ribbon appliqué is that you can keep it simple and sophisticated, or go for the unexpected, in a riot of prints, textures and colours. There are no set rules and it is often surprising to see how attractive colours, interesting weaves and prints can look, even though you would not normally consider putting them together. In short, experiment!

Love Knot Cushion

You will need:
2 $^3/_4$yd (2.5m) printed satin ribbon $^7/_8$in (23mm) wide
1 $^1/_8$yd (1m) fabric 45in (115cm) wide
2/3yd (60cm) contrasting fabric 45in (115cm) wide
1 $^7/_8$yd (1.70m) piping cord
10in (25cm) zip
15in (38cm) square cushion pad

1 Cut two bands on the bias from the contrasting fabric, each measuring 35¼x7¼in (88x18cm). Trim each end to a point, matching the shape of the cushion corner. Cut one cushion front and one cushion back from the other fabric, adding a $^5/_8$in (15mm) seam allowance on all sides.

2 Using a moderate iron, press in the ribbon placement lines on one band as shown. Machine the ribbons in place, taking care not to stretch the bias-cut band.
Tip: Always sew the ribbon edges in the same direction to prevent puckering.

3 With right sides together, machine the two bias bands together, leaving the ends open. Turn to the right side and press. Tie a loose knot in the centre of the band.
Lay the band diagonally across the cushion front, with the knot in the centre and the pointed ends in each corner. Tack each end to the cushion front. Working on the wrong side of the cushion, stitch through to the knot and secure it in place with a few strong stitches.

4 Cut 1 $^1/_4$in (3cm) wide bias strips from the remaining contrast fabric to cover the piping cord. Make a continuous strip, long enough to edge the entire cushion, by joining the pieces as necessary. Press all seams flat. Enclose the piping cord and tack the raw edges together.

5 Place the cord to the cushion front, with raw edges together. Tack in place. With right sides together, machine the cushion front to the back, through all thicknesses. Stitch as close as possible to the piping cord. Leave a gap along one edge for the zip. Turn to the right side and press. Hand stitch the zip in place to complete.

Versailles Rectangular Cushion

You will need:
2 $^5/_8$yd (2.40m) printed satin ribbon $^7/_8$in (23mm) wide
14in (35cm) fabric 45in (115cm) wide for cushion cover
20in (50cm) contrast fabric 45in (115cm) wide for cushion edging
1 $^7/_8$yd (1.70m) piping cord
15in (38cm) zip
Cushion pad 18x12in (45x30cm)

1 Cut out the cushion cover front and back to fit the pad, adding a $^5/_8$in (15mm) seam allowance on all sides.

2 Fold vertical lines on the cushion front and press lightly with a moderate iron. These will act as a guide for the ribbon position.

3 Starting at the centre, tack and machine each ribbon in place. Always sew the ribbon edges in the same direction. You may prefer to use a fabric glue stick instead of tacking.

4 Cut 1 $^1/_4$in (3cm) wide bias strips from the remaining contrast fabric to cover the piping cord. Make a continuous strip, long enough to edge the entire cushion, by joining the pieces as necessary. Press all seams flat. Enclose the piping cord and tack the raw edges together.

5 Place the cord to the cushion front, with raw edges together. Tack in place. With right sides together, machine the cushion front to the back, through all thicknesses. Stitch as close as possible to the piping cord. Leave a gap along one edge for the zip. Turn to the right side and press. Hand stitch the zip in place to complete.

Lattice Work Cushion

You will need:
3 $^{1}/_{8}$yd (2.80m) printed satin ribbon $^{7}/_{8}$in (23mm) wide
14in (35cm) fabric 45in (115cm) wide for cushion cover
20in (50cm) contrast fabric for cushion edging
1 $^{1}/_{2}$yd (1.40m) piping cord
10in (25cm) zip
12 $^{1}/_{2}$in (32cm) square cushion pad

1 Cut out a cushion front and back to fit the pad, adding a seam allowance of $^{5}/_{8}$in (15mm) on all sides. Using the photo as a guide, press vertical and horizontal creases on the cushion front using a moderate iron. These will form the placement lines for the ribbon.

2 Cut the ribbon into eight equal lengths. Place the ribbons on the cushion front one at a time, to achieve the lattice effect. Either tack or lightly glue the ribbon and machine in place, ensuring that you sew all ribbon edges in the same direction.

3 Complete the cushion by following steps 4 and 5 in the Love Knot Cushion instructions.

RIBBON WAISTCOAT

A dashing waistcoat for teddy would look equally splendid scaled up to wear yourself. Co-ordinate the ribbons as we have, in plaids and plains, or try a more haphazard concoction for an eccentric, party look. Easy to make and fun to wear!

For a variation on the theme, weave the waistcoat, using any one of the ribbon weaving techniques outlined on pages 28-31. Our waistcoat is only appliquéd on the front. You could appliqué ribbons to the entire waistcoat.

You will need:
Three contrasting ribbons, all $^{3}/_{8}$in (9mm) wide, numbered 1, 2 and 3:
No 1 - 3 $^{1}/_{4}$yd (3m) tartan taffeta ribbon
No 2 - 2yd (1.80m) plain red satin ribbon
No 3 - 1 $^{5}/_{8}$yd (1.50m) plain blue satin ribbon

Purchased plain waistcoat/vest pattern,* chest size 22–24in (55–60cm)
20in (50cm) medium weight, sew-in interfacing
16in (40cm) lining fabric
16in (40cm) silk dupion
5 $^{1}/_{2}$in (14cm) elastic $^{3}/_{8}$in (9mm) wide
3 buttons

Note: Fabric requirements include a seam allowance of $^{5}/_{8}$in (15mm). Remember to increase ribbon and material requirements for larger sizes.

*See Stockists, page 124, for waistcoat kits.

1 Using the pattern cut the following:
Interfacing: Two fronts
Lining: One back and two fronts
Silk Dupion: One back and belt pieces (if required).

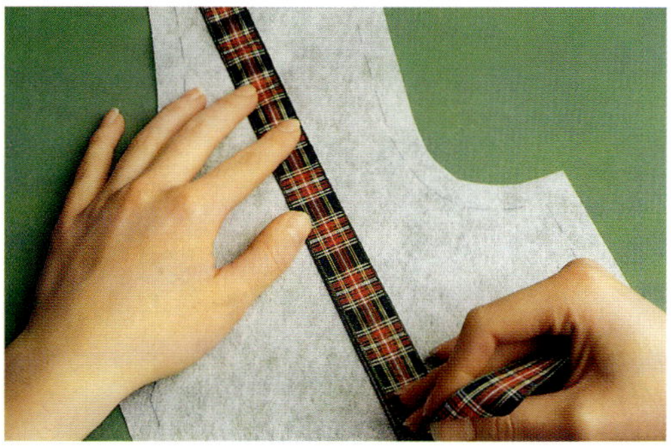

2 Mark a guideline down the centre of each front. With right sides uppermost, place one length of ribbon No 1 on the interfacing along the armhole side of the guideline. Machine in place using a straight stitch and sewing both edges in the same direction to avoid puckering.

Tip: Use a fabric glue stick to hold the ribbon in place before you stitch. Cut out each ribbon strip then position and sew one at a time, rather than all at the same time.

3 Machine ribbon No 3 either side of ribbon No 1, positioning the edges so that they just touch. Next add ribbon No 2 either side, then No 3 and then No 1 again. Continue with this sequence until the front is completely covered with ribbon. Work the second waistcoat front to mirror the first.

Complete the waistcoat following your pattern instructions or those that follow.

4 Fold the waistcoat belt in half along the length, right sides together. Stitch, leaving both ends open. Turn to right side, press. Press the raw edges to the inside at each end. Thread the elastic through, securing at either end with a row of stitching. Stitch the belt to each side of the waistcoat back at the positions marked on the seams.

5 Join the waistcoat back to the fronts at the side seams. Make up the lining in the same way. With right sides together, place lining to waistcoat and stitch around all edges, except the shoulder seams. Turn through to the right side and press.

6 Join the main fabric at the shoulder seams, leaving the lining free. Press the seams flat and then slipstitch the lining in place, covering all raw edges. Make three buttonholes and sew on the buttons to complete the waistcoat.

Ribbon Patchwork

Patchwork is a traditional craft which, in recent years has seen an enormous revival. Originally patchwork was a way to utilize the merest scraps of precious material when re-cycling was very much the order of the day. As fabric became more plentiful, patchwork designs became increasingly intricate and the popularity of the craft soon extended to people in all walks of life.

The method of applying patches to a backing cloth was very popular during the Victorian era, on both sides of the Atlantic. There was a constant exchange of patchwork designs between the Old and New Worlds. The early settlers took their craft with them as they emigrated but over the years patchwork developed into a very distinctive national craft. By the second half of the 19th Century their influence could be clearly seen on British work of that time. In rural districts patchwork was still linked with thrift and economy, but ladies with a more leisurely lifestyle took up patchwork as an alternative to embroidery. They used silks, satins and brocades, which were often embellished with beading and fancy stitches.

Today the techniques involved do not need to be time consuming or complicated, and the pleasure that is derived from making and using something that you have personally made, is worth every effort.

Ribbons can be used successfully for so many strip patchwork designs and the absence of raw edges to finish is a great advantage over other fabrics. Because the patchwork is made by sewing onto a firm foundation fabric, it is quite possible to mix together different ribbon types and weights. The multitude of ribbon colours and designs currently available allows the patchworker to produce results that are always a delight to the eye, and almost always unique. There are numerous ways to arrange the ribbons for patchwork; Log Cabin is probably the most widely known, but Courthouse Steps and Pineapple are equally popular. There is still plenty of scope for experimenting; allow the designs, colours and textures of the ribbons which follow to feed your imagination.

Our quilting project feature three different patchwork techniques. Each technique is quite simple and can be used either singly or collectively to create stunning results that will be treasured favourites for years to come.

There are not many rules in ribbon patchwork. Different people work in different ways; 'right' and 'wrong' do not really apply. In general, use the way of working that suits you best, but accuracy is essential to create patches of an equal size for the three techniques that we are going to use. One of the joys of ribbon patchwork is its adaptability. As you progress from smaller items to more ambitious projects, you will want to create your own designs.

A medium non-woven interfacing is a good and inexpensive backing fabric for the ribbons. If you are careful, you can bond the ribbons in place before you start stitching, using a fabric glue stick or fusible webbing. For crazy patchwork (page 110) you can pin the ribbon to an iron-on interfacing and then bond the ribbons in place before cutting out the random shapes.

Patchwork does not require much in the way of tools and equipment. You probably have most of the essential items in your sewing basket, pins, needle, thread and scissors.

Log Cabin

Log Cabin is one of the oldest recorded types of patchwork. It is known to have been worked in Scotland by at least the middle of the 18th Century, but it has a long tradition on both sides of the Atlantic. The design has been known under several different names, but Log Cabin is the most widely known.

The use of light and dark ribbons, or prints and plains in co-ordinating colours, to frame a small centre square gives a strong three-dimensional effect in this patchwork technique. The strips of ribbon are top-stitched to a foundation fabric, either by hand or machine. No templates are needed and there are no raw edges to deal with; saving a great deal of time and giving a good result. Increase or decrease the size of a project by simply adding or subtracting squares.

This traditional method is very easy and fun to do. Each square is usually divided diagonally with one side worked in paler tones, and one in darker shades.

For a cushion as illustrated, a collection of soft apricots is used tone-on-tone and stitched onto a medium weight interfacing. When the entire area has been worked, the patchwork is mounted on a cream chintz and made into a cushion.

For a 6in (15cm) square you will need: Approximately $2^1/_3$ yd (2.10m) of $^3/_8$in (9mm) ribbon or $1^1/_2$ yd (1.35m) of $^7/_8$in (23mm) ribbon.

1 Cut out squares of medium weight sew-in interfacing. The number and size of the squares will depend upon the finished project size. In this case each square is a quarter of the cushion cover size, i.e. 6in (15cm) square for a finished 12in (30cm) square.

2 Draw diagonal lines from corner to corner on each square, using a pencil and ruler. These markings give a guideline for positioning the ribbon and also provide a centre point.

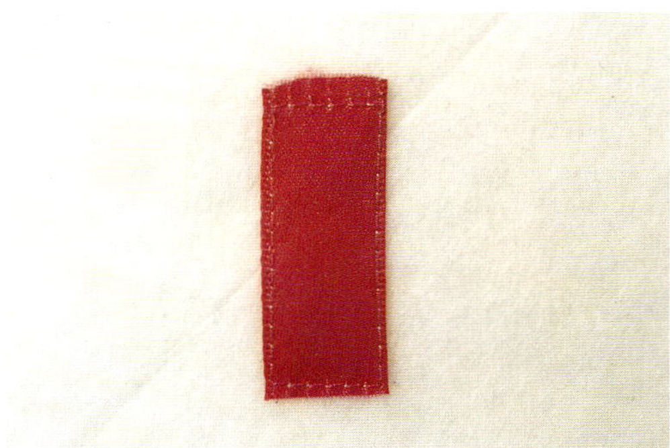

3 Cut a square of ribbon (this is traditionally in a dark or bright colour) and place it centrally over the diagonal intersection. Sew in place.

4 Following the steps illustrated, stitch lengths of the ribbons around the central square, each time overlapping the ends of the previous ribbon to conceal raw ends. Each square is worked in exactly the same way.

5 Join the squares following the technique used in step 10 of the Cot Cover, page 108.

The seam allowance on the ribbon strips can be between $^1/_4$in (7mm) and $^1/_2$in (12mm), depending on what you feel most comfortable with. This will, to some extent, influence the width of ribbon you choose for the patchwork. Pin, tack or glue the ribbons in place until you achieve a degree of expertise. Then you will find that the outer edge of the last ribbon will be your guide.

For the more ambitious, the patchwork squares could be one of many sections that go towards the making of a large quilt. Consider making a whole collection of cushions in your chosen colour scheme, but employing different patchwork or weaving patterns for each one.

Courthouse Steps

A variation on the Log Cabin patchwork, this design is built up around the centre square with pairs of matching ribbons. Vary the effect with the alternate use of light and dark shades in solid colours and prints, but you must always remember to work in pairs.

Pineapple Patchwork

Start with a centre square made up of three vertical ribbons. Place a ribbon diagonally across each corner. Continue with another four ribbons placed around the four sides of the square. Complete this square with another set of diagonal ribbons and so on.

All raw edges will be covered by the next layer of ribbon. When selecting colour for the straight ribbons, choose the same colour or tones within that colour. The diagonals can be in a variety of shades.

A lovely combination of nursery prints, used in traditional patchwork patterns, makes this child's cot cover a wonderful heirloom for future generations.

It is made from seven squares of Courthouse Steps patchwork and eight squares of Pineapple patchwork, which are linked with toning bands of ribbon. The finished size is 40x24in (100x60cm). Wadding or batting may be placed in the cover for additional warmth but, if the cover is intended for a very young baby, do remember to use the correct weight to avoid overheating. Ensure all materials used are fully washable.

Patchwork Cot Cover

You will need:
13yd (12m) cream jacquard ribbon $^3/_8$in (9mm) wide
7 $^1/_2$yd (6.80m) peach floral craft ribbon $^5/_8$in (15mm) wide
5 $^1/_8$yd (4.70m) children's novelty craft ribbon $^5/_8$in (15mm) wide
9 $^1/_2$yd (8.70m) blue duck craft ribbon $^5/_8$in (15mm) wide
5yd (4.50m) peach duck craft ribbon $^5/_8$in (15mm) wide
9yd (8.30m) bluebell doubleface satin ribbon $^7/_8$in (23mm) wide
3 $^7/_8$yd (3.50m) bluebell doubleface satin ribbon 1 $^1/_2$in (39mm) wide
3yd (2.70m) coral doubleface satin ribbon $^7/_8$in (23mm) wide
2 $^1/_4$yd (2.10m) poly cotton backing fabric 36in (90cm) wide
1yd (90cm) square of medium weight, sew-in interfacing
24in (60cm) snap fastener tape
Vanishing fabric marker pen

1 Cut the interfacing into fifteen squares, each measuring 8 $^1/_2$in (21.5cm) square. An allowance of $^3/_4$in (2cm) has been allowed on each square for seams and human error when stitching the ribbon strips. Any extra allowance can be trimmed away later. The finished size of each square will be 7in (17.5cm).

Note: Do not cut the ribbons into lengths before sewing. Cut them as each length has been attached.

Prepare seven squares of Courthouse Steps and eight in the Pineapple design.

2 Pineapple Patchwork Squares
Draw a 1 $^1/_8$in (2.7cm) square in the centre of eight interfacing squares. Machine three

lengths of $^3/_8$in (9mm) cream ribbon across the square, leaving a $^3/_8$in (9mm) seam allowance at each end.

3 Using the marker pen, mark a point $^1/_2$in (12mm) along each side of the square. Sew lengths of $^7/_8$in (23mm) bluebell ribbon diagonally across the centre square corners to form a diamond. The points marked will be the meeting point for the ribbons.

4 Sew lengths of blue duck ribbon in a square across the bluebell diagonals, covering the raw ends of the previous ribbons.

5 Measure $^7/_8$in (23mm) from the edge of the previous bluebell diagonal and sew coral ribbon in a parallel manner over the four corners.

6 Repeat step 4 with the peach duck ribbon. Measure 1 $^1/_4$in (3cm) from the edge of the coral diagonals and stitch bluebell ribbon down in diagonals.

7 Stitch down blue duck as step 4. Complete eight squares of patchwork in this design.

8 Courthouse Steps Patchwork
Take the remaining seven interfacing squares and draw a $^7/_8$in (23mm) square in the centre. Machine a length of coral ribbon to this square, leaving $^3/_8$in (9mm) at each end.

9 Stitch down the ribbons in the following sequence, always ensuring that you sew matching ribbons to the opposite side of the centre square: one cream, one novelty print, one cream, one floral peach. Repeat this sequence three times so that you have three cream ribbons and three print ribbons on each side of the centre square.

Complete all seven squares in this manner. Trim the interfacing allowance on all fifteen squares to $^3/_8$in (9mm).

10 Cut the backing fabric into three pieces; two measuring 40x24in (100x60cm) and one 4x24in (10x60cm). Alternating the patchwork styles, place the patchwork pieces onto one large piece of the backing fabric. Leave a $^7/_8$in (23mm) space between each square. Make sure all the edges line up. Machine the squares in place around all edges, then machine the narrow bluebell ribbon vertically and horizontally between the patchwork pieces. Butt the ribbon edges firmly together.

11 Take the second large piece of fabric and turn a hem across one width. Do the same on the shorter piece of fabric. Attach the snap fastener tape to the two separate pieces of fabric along the width. Fasten the snaps so that the two fabrics now act as one piece. With wrong sides together, tack the quilt front and back together along all raw edges.

12 Place a length of the 1 $^1/_2$in (39mm) bluebell ribbon along one edge of the quilt back so that the ribbon edge lies $^5/_8$in (15mm) in from the raw edges of the fabric. Machine in place then fold the ribbon over to the front and machine again on the quilt front. Bind the other three edges in the same manner but leave $^3/_8$in (9mm) extra at each end on the short edges. Fold this allowance under to neaten the raw edges.

Crazy Patchwork Shawl

Crazy patchwork was much loved by ladies in the late Victorian era when off-cuts from dressmaking were plentiful. You can achieve the same effect today with satin, velvet, moiré and jacquard ribbons. With all the advantages of modern technology, your crazy patchwork will be less fragile than the few Victorian samples which still survive today.

This type of patchwork, in common with Log Cabin, Courthouse Steps and Pineapple, requires no templates. The ribbons are first bonded to a long piece of fusible webbing, then cut into random shapes before being applied in a jig-saw puzzle fashion to a backing fabric. Once the whole surface is covered, the patchwork edges are concealed and stablized with another ribbon, braid or surface embroidery.

The deep, rich colours of green and burgundy, scattered with black, in a variety of equally rich textures, give a Victorian look to this crazy patchwork. Don the shawl for elegant eveningwear, or use the piece as a casual throw which sits comfortably on a favourite armchair or sofa. If you prefer a more contemporary style, use a riotous collection of colours and top-stitch in bright silks.

Scale: 1 square = 2 in (5 cm)

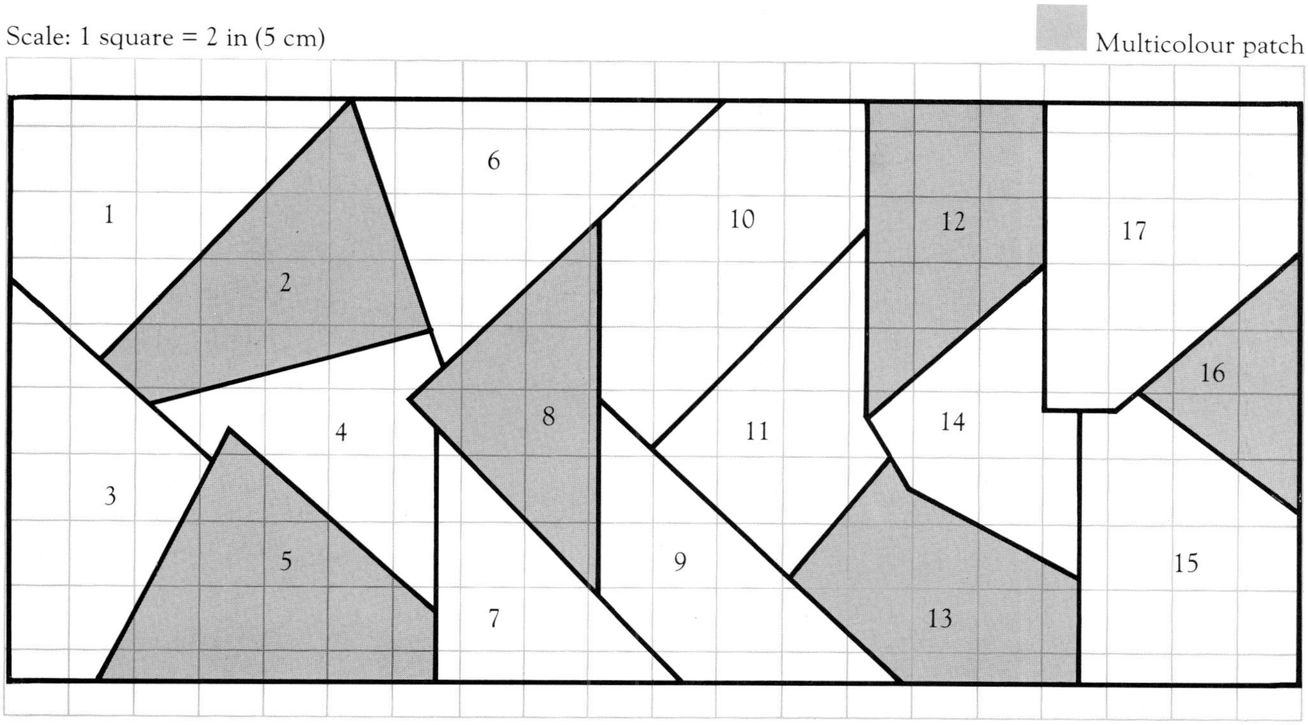

For a finished piece, measuring 18x40in (45x100cm), you will need:
A selection of black ribbons in different widths and textures; satin, taffeta, grosgrain, jacquard etc. to cover an area 20x40in (50x100cm).
A selection of green, purple and wine-coloured ribbons to cover an area 10x32in (25x80cm).
3 $^{1}/_{4}$yd (3m) of 1 $^{1}/_{2}$in (39mm) wide ribbon to edge the shawl
Fusible webbing 30x36in (75x90cm)
Black backing fabric 40x18in (100x45cm) wide
Needle and sewing thread
Pinboard

1 The patchwork is prepared in two steps. First you will make large areas of ribbon appliqué, which will then be cut into the smaller shapes to create the patchwork shown on the chart. Start by cutting the webbing into three pieces, each 10x36in (25x90cm).

2 Take the first piece and lay it on the pinboard. Pin lines of assorted black ribbons to the webbing. Repeat this on the second piece of webbing. Pin rows of coloured ribbon to the third piece of webbing. Pin at both ends of the ribbon and butt each piece tightly up against the adjacent ribbon. Once each webbing piece is complete, iron on the ribbon side, following the manufacturer's instructions, to fuse.

3 Now you are ready to cut out the patchwork shapes from the three pieces of webbing. Follow the chart for guidance or cut out your own shapes, bearing in mind each shape you have to fill as you cut. Minimize waste by cutting and positioning one shape at a time.

4 Lay the shapes down on the wrong side of the backing fabric, ribbon work uppermost. Starting at one corner, overlap or butt each shape together and tack in place. Try to distribute the coloured and plain patches evenly.

5 Stitch over all the edges, either by hand or machine using decorative stitches such as herringbone, feather stitch or zigzag. Remove tacking and iron carefully, fusing the second side of the webbing to the backing fabric.

6 Take the edging ribbon and fold it in half lengthways, wrong sides together. Press. This foldline will help you to achieve a symmetrical finish on both sides of the throw. Now bind all the edges, mitering the ribbon at each corner. Machine or hand stitch.

Tip: Velvet is very effective but quite difficult to fuse to the backing fabric, so use only a small amount and place it carefully.

Silk Blind

In shot silk, appliquéd with metallic-edged sheer ribbon for subtle definition, this roller blind is both functional and sophisticated. The appliquéd patterning can be as simple or as complex as you wish. The same ribbon can also be used for decorative roses and bows on co-ordinating soft furnishings.

For a blind with a finished size of 43x58in (110x146.5cm) you will need:
4 $^{3}/_{8}$yd (4m) sheer ribbon with metallic edge 1 $^{1}/_{2}$in (39mm) wide
8 $^{3}/_{4}$yd (8m) sheer ribbon with metallic edge $^{5}/_{8}$in (15mm) wide
1 $^{5}/_{8}$yd (1.50m) silk dupion 44in (112cm) wide
Purchased roller blind kit
Needle and sewing thread
Ruler
Waterproof black marker pen
Tracing paper 60x46in (150x114cm)
Vanishing fabric marker pen

1 Cut the fabric to 44x58in (111x146cm) Turn a $^{1}/_{2}$in (12mm) hem allowance to the right side, down either side of the blind. Press.

2 Using the scale drawing and waterproof marker pen, transfer the appliqué pattern to the tracing paper. Place this, right side up, on a large, flat work surface. Carefully pin the blind, right side up, on top of this. Using the vanishing marker pen, trace the pattern onto the silk. Separate the tracing paper and blind.

3 Now pin the 1 $^{1}/_{2}$in (39mm) ribbon to the blind; starting at the top right hand corner and using the ribbon in one continuous strip on the right side of the fabric. Follow the direction arrows on the chart, folding the ribbon where necessary. Machine along the

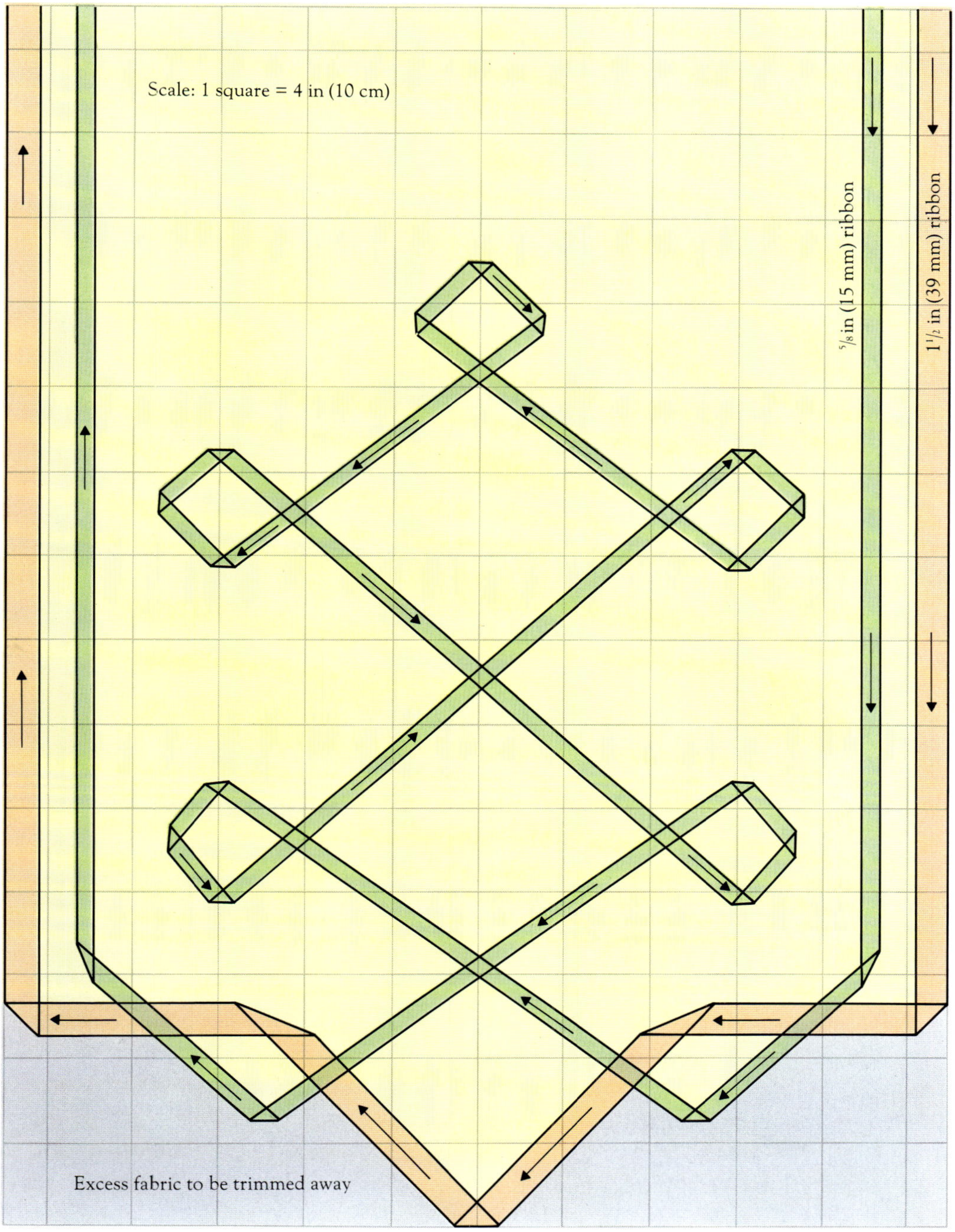

You will find it easier to transfer the appliqué ribbon pattern if you select a translucent fabric for the blind.

outside edge of the ribbon, enclosing the side hem allowance, and then along the inner edge. Always sew the two edges of any ribbon in the same direction to avoid puckering.

4 Using the same method, apply the $^5/_8$*in (15mm) ribbon to the blind. Remember to follow the direction arrows for the correct sequence of laying down the ribbon. Machine stitch.*

5 Trim the lower edge of the blind to within $^1/_2$*in(12mm) of the ribbon. Turn this allowance to the wrong side and hand stitch to the blind to secure. Do not stitch through to the ribbon. Clip and ease the corners where necessary. Turn under the hem allowance at the upper edge and machine in place.*

6 Mount the blind on a purchased roller, following the manufacturer's instructions.

Trimmed Bed Linen

A contemporary designer look is achieved on plain bedlinen by the simple addition of appliquéd ribbons. An attractive combination of plaid ribbon linked with a narrow plain ribbon gives the impression of tricky interlacing, which in fact could not be simpler to do!

The use of a narrow width bonding web, for example hemming web, makes for speedy appliqué without a lot of labourious machine work!

For a single sheet, 70in (178cm) wide, you will need:
4yd (3.70m) plaid ribbon $^7/_8$in (23mm) wide
13yd (12m) light navy doubleface satin ribbon $^1/_8$in (3mm) wide
Strip of lightweight iron-on interfacing 4x70in (10x178cm)
Fusible hemming web
Thread to match the ribbon

Note: Measure the width of the sheet and pillowcase to check plaid ribbon quantities required. It is advisable to purchase extra of the narrow ribbon.

For a single pillowcase 20in (50cm) wide you will need:
1 $^1/_4$yd (1.10m) plaid ribbon $^7/_8$in (23mm) wide
2 $^1/_4$yd (2m) light navy doubleface satin ribbon $^1/_8$in (3mm) wide
Strip of lightweight iron-on interfacing 3x20in (7.5x50cm)
Fusible hemming web
Thread to match the ribbon

You will have to undo the side seams of the pillowcase before starting the ribbon work. Turn the pillowcase inside out and the flap over, to enable the stitching to be

unpicked and thus release the flap. Take care to note the position of the flap for reconstruction once the appliqué work is complete.

1 Press the interfacing strips to the wrong side of the sheet and pillowcase, just below the wide stitched hem, using a damp cloth and moderate iron. This is an optional step which will provide a firmer foundation for the appliqué work.

2 Cut the fusible web so that it is slightly narrower than the ribbon width. Following the manufacturer's instructions, fix the plaid ribbon in place with the fusible web. Take care that the pattern of the plaid on the two rows is in line.

For the sheet; place one length of ribbon on the right side, covering the hem stitches and another length 2 $^{1}/_{2}$in (6.5cm) from the first. Turn the ribbon ends under at the side edges.

For the pillowcase; place the two rows of ribbon using the same method. Leave a space of 1 $^{3}/_{4}$in (4.5cm) between the two rows. Place the raw edges within the seam allowance.

3 Machine along the ribbon edges with a small zigzag stitch, always working in the same direction to avoid puckering.

4 Machine the narrow ribbon between the two rows of plaid, using a zigzag stitch again. Choosing a guide-line on the plaid pattern, hold the ribbon in place diagonally between the two rows and machine down the centre of the ribbon. Leave the needle in the fabric as you turn the work and the ribbon between the rows. Turn the ribbon edges under as you start and finish machining the narrow ribbon on the sheet.

5 Press the ribbon with a damp cloth and moderate iron. Join the side seams of the pillowcase again, with right sides together and the flap over. Turn to the right side and press.

Plaid Pillow

Why not make a cluster of cushions to sit on the bed for a totally co-ordinated look?

For one 15in (38cm) cushion you will need:
$^{7}/_{8}$yd (80cm) red plaid ribbon 1 $^{1}/_{2}$in (39mm) wide
1 $^{1}/_{2}$yd (1.40m) plain red ribbon $^{5}/_{8}$in (15mm) wide
1 $^{1}/_{2}$yd (1.40m) green plaid ribbon $^{7}/_{8}$in (23mm) wide
2 $^{1}/_{8}$yd (1.95m) plain green ribbon $^{3}/_{8}$in (9mm) wide
2 $^{1}/_{4}$yd (2m) red ribbon $^{3}/_{16}$in (5mm) wide
2 $^{1}/_{4}$yd (2m) blue ribbon $^{1}/_{4}$in (7mm) wide
1 $^{1}/_{4}$yd (1.10m) blue plaid ribbon $^{7}/_{8}$in (23mm)

$^{5}/_{8}$yd (50cm) fabric 48in (120cm) wide
15 $^{5}/_{8}$in (39cm) square of lightweight iron-on interfacing
Dressmakers' squared pattern paper 18in (45cm) square (optional)
Fusible hemming web

$1\ ^{3}/_{4}$yd (1.60m) piping cord
Sewing thread to match the fabric
12in (30cm) snap fastener tape
Cushion pad 15in (38cm) square
Pinboard

Tip: Always trim the fusible web so that it is slightly narrower than the ribbon width.

Note: A seam allowance of $^{5}/_{8}$in (15mm) has been included on all fabric requirements.

1 Cut a 15 $^{5}/_{8}$in (39cm) square of fabric for the cushion front and a piece 18 $^{5}/_{8}$x15 $^{5}/_{8}$in (46.5x39cm) for the cushion back. Stabilize the appliqué by fusing the lightweight interfacing to the wrong side of the cushion front, using a damp cloth and moderate iron. Allow to cool. Fold the cushion front into four and lightly crease with an iron; thus providing the guidelines to ensure a symmetrical finish. Alternatively use the squared paper behind the cushion front as a guideline. Pin the prepared cushion front to the pinboard.

2 Make up the appliqué centre square by cutting four equal lengths of the 1 $^{1}/_{2}$in (39mm) plaid ribbon. Join the ribbon corners together with the fusible web, following the manufacturer's instructions.

3 Place the prepared plaid ribbon to the cushion front, making sure it is squarely in position. Secure in place with fusible web. Place the other ribbons diagonally in sequence as shown in the photograph. Fuse the red ribbon and the green plaid one piece at a time. The three narrow ribbons can all be fused in place at the same time. When all the ribbons are in place give a final press on the right side with a moderate iron and damp cloth. Allow to cool. If using the squared paper, remove before pressing.

4 Cut bias strips 1 $^{1}/_{4}$in (3cm) wide, from the remaining fabric. Join together to give a length of 64in (160cm). Cover the piping cord with this strip. It is easier to stitch the cord cover with a zip foot. Pin, then stitch the piping to the cushion front, using the $^{3}/_{8}$in (9mm) seam allowance. The two ends of cord should be joined as neatly as possible.

5 Fold the cushion backing fabric in half along the longest edge and cut, giving two pieces. Turn in a single hem of 1in (2.5cm) along both cut edges. Zigzag to neaten and press. Overlap the two edges and attach the snap fastener tape. When fastened, the cushion back should be the same size as the cushion front. With right sides together, machine the front to the back around all four sides. Trim and clip the seam where necessary. Turn to the right side and press. Insert the cushion pad.

VELVET BAUBLES

This simple idea is a starting point for all kinds of decorations. Dried berries, flower-heads and leaves can all be combined with the ribbons. The heraldic colours of deep velvets with gold grosgrain make for a lovely collection to display in a bowl as a cheery mid-winter decoration. Fresh spring pastels could be used for a completely different look as the seasons change.

White polystyrene balls are used as the base. They should be tightly covered with the decoration to prevent the white showing through.

To make one of each design you will need:
Gold metallic grosgrain ribbon $^1/_8$in (3mm) wide
Gold metallic grosgrain ribbon $^3/_8$in (9mm) wide
$^1/_4$in (7mm) wide velvet ribbon in each of the following colours: gold, purple, scarlet, moss green and chocolate
Polystyrene balls, approximately 3in (7.5cm) diameter
Gold lace pins
Scissors

Quarter Patterned Ball

1 Divide the ball into four equal segments with the $^1/_8$in (3mm) gold ribbon, overlapping and pinning the ends neatly. Cut the velvet ribbons into suitable lengths and, using the previously pinned gold ribbon as a guide, lay a colour pattern over the ball. Alternate the direction of the ribbons in each section. Pin the cut ends neatly, aligning the pin heads.

2 Using a $^3/_8$in (9mm) gold grosgrain, cover the pins along each segment and pin securely to finish.

Striped Ball

Encircle a polystrene ball with a sequence of velvet ribbons in various colours, alternated with gold grosgrain. Pin neatly at the top and bottom of the base where the colours cross. Ensure the ribbon fits snugly to the ball.

CLOVE BALLS

For an aromatic decoration, herbs and spices can be integrated with the ribbon to form part of the design. They serve two purposes; they are ornamental and could be placed in wardrobes or drawers to scent lingerie and other clothing. Cloves have been traditionally used as a moth deterrent.

For each ball you will need:
1 $^5/_8$yd (1.50m) gold metallic grosgrain ribbon $^1/_8$in (3mm) wide
28in (72cm) velvet ribbon $^1/_4$in (7mm) wide
Polystyrene ball approximately 2in (5cm) diameter
Whole cloves
Gold lace pins

1 Take the velvet ribbon and encircle the ball. Pin the overlap neatly and cut off the remaining ribbon. The ball is now divided into two. Repeat this step three times, dividing the ball into eight equal sectors. Lay a band of gold grosgrain to either side of each velvet circle, always pinning neatly at the top and bottom.

2 Closely stud the eight narrow sectors between the grosgrain bands with the cloves, making sure that the end cloves are equidistant from the top and bottom.

GLOSSARY

Woven-Edge

This ribbon is woven as a narrow fabric, with two selvege edges. As the popularity of decorative crafts grows, so the range of woven-edge ribbons increases. Many woven-edge ribbons now have a wire-edge and some are embossed or otherwise finished for craft purposes. It cannot be assumed that all are washable or dry cleanable.

Wire-Edge Woven

A fine, flexible wire is woven along the selvege during manufacture, giving this ribbon type the ability to hold a shape when used for creating bows, loops and roses.

Satin

Shiny satins are easy to handle and ideal for ribbon weaving and appliqué work. They are available in plain colours as well as prints; special edging effects include picot or feather-edge and metallic edge.

Satins are either singleface, that is, they are shiny on one side and matt on the other, or doubleface, having a shiny appearance on both sides.

Taffeta

A matt finish is most common in taffeta which is finely woven and the same on both sides. As well as plain colours there are plaids, checks, stripes and more unusual looks. These include ombré, which is colour shading across the width, and shot effects which are achieved in the production process by using different colours for the warp and weft. Moiré taffeta is the result of a shimmering watermark finish during manufacture.

Grosgrain

Available in solid colours, or prints and stripes which are usually woven into the ribbon. An interesting variation to look out for is the satin edge with a grosgrain centre. Grosgrains have a distinctive crosswise rib and you will find they are stronger and denser in handle than the satin or taffeta ribbon.

Jacquards

Florals, small geometrics or ethnic patterning are woven in, giving a surface texture and tone-on-tone effect when a single colour is used. Some jacquards incorporate several colours and have a beautiful tapestry appearance.

Twill

A matt finish in a close weave which is available in both cotton and polyester. This quality has a natural look and is ideal for projects needing a ribbon that is neither shiny or showy.

Sheers

Sheer ribbon can be printed or plain and may incorporate a metallic or satin stripe. They are fine, almost transparent, and make wonderful loops and bows.

On many sheers and other fine ribbons, a thicker thread is woven along the edges to give stability. This is known as a monofilament edge.

Velvet

There is no mistaking the deep rich colour and distinctive plush pile of velvet ribbon. It is available in widths from $^{3}/_{16}$in (5mm) right through to 3 $^{1}/_{4}$in (80mm). There is also a velvet tubing on the market which is useful for a variety of soft crafts.

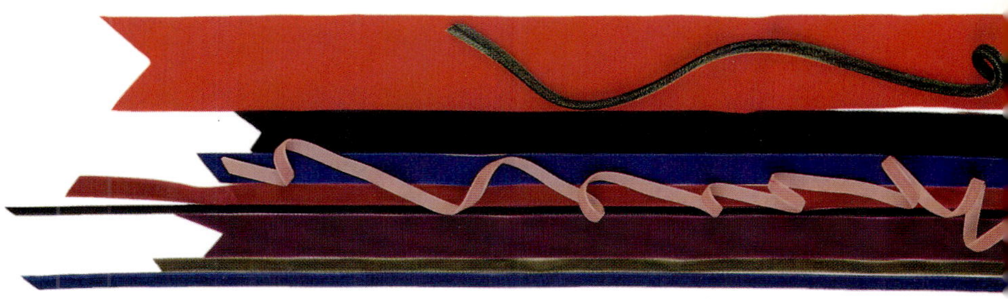

Metallics and Iridescents

Perfect for eveningwear and festive occasions, these are made from metallic or pearlized fibres, sometimes inter-woven with other fibres. Using different weaves and finishes during production, many new looks have been created.

Embellished, Pearled or Gathered

The addition of lace or pearls to a basic ribbon makes for an elaborate, special occasion trim. Satins and sheers are sometimes pre-gathered or pleated, which gives wonderful texture and flexibility.

Cut-Edge or Craft Ribbon

This type of ribbon is made from a wide fabric which is cut into strips of the required ribbon width. It has a special finish which gives the ribbon substance and prevents it from fraying when cut. It is due to this finish that craft ribbons are not normally washable; do check before using them on clothes or soft furnishings.

Wire-Edge Craft Ribbon

As the name suggests, these are made by fusing a wire along the cut-edge of a craft ribbon or fusing the wire into a seam made along the edge of the ribbon.

Merrowed-Edge Craft Ribbon

This is the name given to a fine, satin stitched edge that is applied to more elaborate ribbons made from fabrics such as brocade and silk. Merrowing gives a luxurious finishing touch to these exotic fabrics without affecting their beautiful lustre and handling qualities.

Ribbon Width

From as narrow as $^1/_{16}$in (1.5mm), to 3 $^1/_4$in (80mm) and wider, there is a great deal of choice. So much depends on the scale and application, but most widths are standard throughout the ribbon industry.

Ribbons are sold by the metre or yard, and in pre-cut, packaged lengths. Use the chart to check your ribbon width. It is intended as a guideline only, you may find slight differences among the widths given by individual ribbon manufacturers.

Imperial	Metric	Imperial	Metric
$^1/_{16}$in	1.5mm	1 $^3/_8$in	36mm
$^1/_8$in	3mm	1 $^1/_2$in	39mm
$^3/_{16}$in	5mm	2in	50mm
$^1/_4$in	7mm	2 $^1/_4$in	56mm
$^3/_8$in	9mm	2 $^5/_8$in	67mm
$^1/_2$in	12mm	2 $^3/_4$in	70mm
$^5/_8$in	15mm	3in	77mm
$^7/_8$in	23mm	3 $^1/_4$in	80mm

All the ribbons featured in Practical Ribboncraft projects are from the Offray and Lion Ribbon range.

In business since 1876, and now probably the world's largest ribbon manufacturer, Offray is still a family-run business; the grandfather of the current Offray President was the original founder of the company.

Offray now boasts factories, warehouses, showrooms and offices throughout the United States of America, Canada and Europe where the latest technology is employed to produce a dazzling selection of ribbons.

In recent years Offray acquired Lion Ribbon, a market leader in ribbons for the craft and floral markets. This acquisition brought together two very well-known brand names of international repute and today their products are easily obtained from numerous stores and specialist outlets.

Stockists and Suppliers

Ribboncraft equipment, ribbons, haberdashery and miscellaneous craft items used in Practical Ribboncrafts, have been obtained from the following sources:

Bonbonnière equipment and mail order ribbon:
Rainbow Ribbons
Unit D5 Seedbed Centre
Davidson Way
Romford
Essex RM7 OAZ

Bowmakers, Weaving Boards and assorted Ribboncraft Kits:
Ribbon Renaissance
57 Kiln Ride
Wokingham
Berkshire RG11 3PJ

Bowmakers (USA):
Bond America
435 Seventh Avenue
Brooklyn
NY 11215

Cake Decorating Supplies:
Squires Kitchen
Squires House
3 Waverley Lane
Farnham
Surrey GU9 8BB

Craft Supplies:
Peter Harvey Floral Art Products Ltd
Albany House
Leigh Street
High Wycombe
Buckinghamshire HP11 2QU

Embroidery Thread/Cloth:
Coats Patons Crafts
McMullen Road
Darlington
Co Durham DL1 1YQ

Coats & Clark Inc
Coats Crafts North America
30 Patwood Drive
Suite 351
Greenville SC29615

DMC Creative World
Pulham Road
Wigston
Leicestershire LE18 2DY

DMC Corporation
Port Kearny
Building 10
South Kearny NJ 07032

Fabric Glue Stick & Thread:
Perivale-Gütermann Ltd
Wadsworth Road
Greenford
Middlesex UB6 7JS

Gütermann of America Inc
PO Box 7387
Charlotte NC 28241

Hat Boxes:
Woking Tube Products
London NW10

Interfacings and fusible webbing:
Freudenberg Nonwovens Ltd
Vilene Retail
PO Box 3, Greetland
Halifax HX4 8NJ
West Yorkshire

Carl Freudenberg
6940 Weinheim/Bergstrasse
Postfach 1369
Germany

Freudenberg Nonwovens Ltd
Pellon Division
1040 Avenue of the Americas
New York NY 100018

Low-Melt Glue Guns:
Weycraft (TM) Ltd
PO Box 49
Godalming
Surrey GU8 5YX

Mail Order Ribbons and Kits:
Ribbon Designs
42 Lake View
Edgeware
Middlesex HA8 7RU

Patchwork equipment/Haberdashery:
Newey Goodman Ltd
Sedgley Road West
Tipton
West Midlands DY4 8AH

Dritz Corporation
Box 5028
Spartanburg SC 29304

Polystyrene Baubles, Pins
Pinflair
Unit 6
Brew House Lane
Hertford
Herts SG14 2AN

Ribbons:
C M Offray & Son Ltd
Fir Tree Place
Church Road
Ashford
Middlesex TW15 2PH

C M Offray & Son Inc
Route 24
PO BOx 601
Chester
New Jersey 07930 0601

Acknowledgements

I would like to give a special thank you to my family for their constant love and support, especially my husband John, who prevented our home from deteriorating into utter chaos while I was working on the book.

To Julie, who did a magnificent job editing all the copy, and produced a beautiful baby boy in the middle of it all; a real superwoman!

Mary, who was always there to help and advise me, casting her professional eye over the copy time and again.

To the team at Anaya, especially Carey, who made it all happen.

To Claude Offray, who has always been a great support and inspiration and provided all the beautiful ribbons that made this book possible.

To Mark for his wonderful photography.

Finally, and certainly not least, to all my friends who made many of the lovely projects featured in this book. Their constant inter-action creates the perfect environment for new and exciting ideas to grow.

The projects featured in Practical Ribboncraft were designed and made by:

Jenny Banham
Ribbon Appliquéd Waistcoat, Cot Cover, Silk Blind and all featured cushions

Marilyn Becker
Embroidered Needlecase

Caroline Birkett-Harris
Flower Hat Box, Découpage Hat Box, Ribbon Sampler, Victorian Purse and Crazy Patchwork Shawl

Barbara Carpenter
Heart Sachet and Sweetheart Box

Myra Davidson
Trimmed Bedlinen and Plaid Pillow

Sue Hodges
Celebration Cake

Elizabeth Ireland
Vase of Pansies, Napkin and Ring

Pat Isaacs
Plaid Christmas Baubles and Embroidered Picture Frame

Linda Rendina
Table Centrepiece and Wreath

Rita Snelling
Bonbonnières

Mary Straka
Tassels, Drawstring Purses, Cinammon Bundles, Clove Balls and Gift Packaging projects

All other projects designed and made by Christine Kingdom.

INDEX

B

C

D

F

G

H

L

N

P